A POC... ...JTORY

OF ULSTER

**An up-to-date account of the history of
one of the world's most troubled arenas.**

This guide covers the complicated origins, causes and
course of Northern Irish history and traces the roots of the
social divide from early settlement to the emergence of
nationalism and unionism; from the setting up of the
northern state to its descent into instability; from Civil Rights
movement and internment to the ceasefire of 1994.

BRIAN BARTON lectures in History at Queen's University, Belfast, and is an author and expert on Northern Irish history and politics.

A POCKET HISTORY
OF ULSTER

Brian Barton

THE O'BRIEN PRESS
DUBLIN

First published 1996 by The O'Brien Press Ltd.,
20 Victoria Road, Rathgar, Dublin 6, Ireland.
Tel. +353 1 4923333 Fax. +353 1 4922777
e-mail: books@obrien.ie
http://www.obrien.ie
Reprinted 1999

ISBN 0-86278-629-0

A catalogue reference for this title is available
from the British Library

2   3   4   5   6   7   8 9 10
99 00 01 02 03 04 05

The O'Brien Press receives
assistance from

The Arts Council
An Chomhairle Ealaíon

Typesetting, editing, layout, design:
The O'Brien Press Ltd.
Cover photography: Alan O'Connor
Cover separations: C&A Print Services, Dublin
Printing: Guernsey Press Co. Ltd.

ACKNOWLEDGEMENTS

Front cover painting: Smithfield Market, Belfast
(detail) by Cyril Clarke. Photograph reproduced with
kind permission of the Trustees of the National
Museums & Galleries of Northern Ireland.
Back cover painting: The Flax Pullers by Lilian Lucy
Davidson, courtesy of the Brian P. Burns collection.
Photographs from the Public Record Office of
Northern Ireland appear courtesy of the Deputy
Keeper of the Records. I wish also to thank John
Killen, Linen Hall Library, David Miller, *Belfast
Telegraph*, and finally David Bigger, for
providing illustrative material.

Contents

To Valerie, Deirdre and Allen

INTRODUCTION

Any book on Northern Ireland, from its creation in 1921 to the present day, should begin with a caveat. For the past twenty-five years, the statelet, a province of the United Kingdom, has been in a state of political flux and a definitive description of its constitutional position has become increasingly difficult to make. Now, more than ever before, its future is uncertain, and it is impossible to predict what shape it will take. As these pages are being printed, another major effort is in progress to determine its constitutional position and so solve some of the problems which have kept its people in turmoil for three-quarters of a century. Indeed, the troubles of the island of which Northern Ireland is part stretch back for eight hundred years before that. It is said with truth that Ireland is a small island with a big history and, both internally and externally, that history has generally been a difficult and contentious one.

Northern Ireland, therefore, cannot be written about without constant reference to the other part of the island, the Republic of Ireland; nor can either part of the island be considered other than in relation to its connection with Britain. To understand what is happening in Northern Ireland politics now, it is essential to put it into the context of the long and unhappy saga of Anglo-Irish relations. A visitor to Belfast will appreciate this as soon as he sees the flags of two different countries sticking out of the windows in different parts of the city and is faced with murals indicating allegiance to either the United Kingdom or to a united and independent Ireland. This division is deeply-rooted in both of Northern Ireland's communities. The majority of the 1.5 million people in the province give their spiritual allegiance to the Protestant (mainly Presbyterian, Church of Ireland and Methodist) religion and their political loyalty to Queen Elizabeth II. The half-million minority are mainly Catholics and aspire, with varying degrees of enthusiasm, to a thirty-two county, independent Ireland.

This book sets out to explain the nature of these two communities, their origins, their development, their divisions, their objectives. It describes the foundation of the Northern Ireland state and the political and social consequences which sprang from it. It charts the area's changing relationships with Britain and the Irish Republic and explores the influence of the governments in London and Dublin on events in the North. It examines the aims of the organisations, both legal and illegal, which have so affected life in Northern Ireland during the greater part of this century and considers the possible outcome of the present efforts to solve its many problems.

These efforts are the latest – and perhaps the last – in a long series of attempts to bring peace to an island partioned by an act of parliament at Westminster in 1920. The current developments, whether they are confined to political talks or are accompanied by another eruption of violence, may pave the way to eventual unity of the whole island; they may collapse and trigger more of what are euphemistically called 'the Troubles' or they may end in the Northern minority's acceptance, even if temporarily, of the *status quo*. The caveat mentioned above cannot be ignored.

In conclusion, I wish only to express my most profound gratitude to my publishers, The O'Brien Press, whose expertise and encouragement were crucial in shaping the present volume.

Brian Barton
June 1996

CHAPTER 1

The Roots of the Problem

The roots of Irish opposition to British rule and of the current political problems of both parts of Ireland go back over eight centuries to the first English invasions under Strongbow and his Norman knights in 1170. In almost every generation between then and the present, armed insurrections against British rule, sometimes with aid from Spain, France or Rome took place. The old Celtic order, with its clans, minor kings and common land ownership, its Catholic religion and its own language and customs was gradually suppressed and disappeared almost entirely after the Flight of the Earls – the departure of the last of the Irish chieftains and their followers to sanctuary in Europe after their disastrous defeat in 1603. In 1782, British rule was thought to be stable enough to permit the establishment of a separate Irish parliament in Dublin but this was abolished again in 1800 when the Act of Union set up the United Kingdom of Great Britain and Ireland.

From 1 January 1801 until 1921, the whole country was ruled directly from Westminster, where Ireland was represented in the British House of Commons by some hundred members of parliament (MPs) and in the House of Lords by thirty peers. During this time, the seeds of modern Irish nationalism were sown. The movement took two forms – constitutional efforts to secure varying degrees of political independence (Home Rule, as it was called) and complete independence to be won by military means.

The physical force nationalists drew their inspiration from the United Irishmen rebellion of 1798, the Young

Irelanders rebellion of 1848 and the Fenian or Irish Republican Brotherhood rebellion of 1867. They sought a fully independent thirty-two county republic to be achieved by force but their movement had little impact before the Easter Rising in 1916.

Home Rule Movement

Meanwhile, constitutional nationalists formed non-violent, open political organisations, which sought change peacefully through legislation at Westminster. By this means they hoped to attain a limited measure of self-government for Ireland. The Home Rule movement, founded in 1869, was the most effective of these and was very nearly successful. Its growth was partly due to the charismatic leadership provided by Charles Stewart Parnell, a Protestant landowner from County Wicklow. Under his guidance, it exploited and stimulated a greater political consciousness amongst the Irish people. It championed and articulated popular grievances – particularly those of the tenant farmers, amongst whom the unpredictability of rents aroused widespread fear of eviction. Through highly effective organisation, it mobilised the Irish electorate, which trebled in 1884 as a result of franchise reform. By then, the Home Rule Party returned over eighty MPs to Westminster and was the first truly modern political party to be represented there. Its political leaders were salaried and it had an effective network of constituency branches throughout Ireland.

The Origins of Ulster Unionism

As nationalists, who were mainly Catholics, struggled to win freedom for all Ireland by force or by persuasion, the mainly Protestant population of Northern Ireland strove just as strongly to preserve intact the union with Britain. Unionist leaders sought to convince the British parliament and people that it would be unwise and unjust to grant Irish self-government.

Until the 1880s Northern Ireland Protestants, like their Catholic fellow-countrymen, were also divided. They were split along political lines, the more conservative group supporting the British Conservative Party, others the Liberals. They also belonged to different social classes. Some were land-owning aristocrats, others the tenants who coveted their land. Some were wealthy industrialists, others the factory workers whom they exploited and underpaid. There were even inter-denominational distinctions and tensions – in particular between Church of Ireland members (until 1869 Ireland's established church) and the more numerous Presbyterians, who resented the residual trappings and airs of privilege of the others. It was the deep-seated fear and alarm shared by almost all Protestants at the prospect of Dublin (and Rome) rule which enabled them to overcome their differences.

In mid-1885, in direct response to growing nationalist agitation, the Irish Protestants set out to construct a strong, united movement in Ireland itself. Though it originated in Dublin, its most fervent support (then as now) came from the 890,000 Protestants living in Ulster, where they comprised 57 percent of the population. Elsewhere in the country, unionism failed to attract the votes of more than 10 percent of the electorate.

A Protestant Majority

The supporters of unionism strove to preserve the Union with Britain for a variety of reasons. In part they

13

did so because they felt a positive and instinctive loyalty towards Britain and valued the security of belonging to a Protestant majority in the United Kingdom, as opposed to being part of a minority in a predominantly Catholic, self-governing Ireland. This reflected their sense of their own national distinctiveness; they differed from the majority population not just in religion but in culture, ethnic origins and political aspirations.

Above all else, unionists were convinced that Ireland had benefited materially from the union; in the northeast, this seemed evident. During the nineteenth century, the population of Belfast had increased eighteen-fold owing to rapid industrialisation, in particular the growth of linen manufacture, shipbuilding, engineering and rope-making. Though the city contained just one-fifth of the population of Ireland in 1900, it produced one-third of its total manufacturing output and accounted for two-thirds of its industrial exports. Local Protestant businessmen attributed this startling economic expansion not just to their own commercial skills and flair but also, crucially, to the political link with Britain. They were acutely conscious of their dependence on British markets, raw materials, capital and even skilled labour supplies and, in some notable instances, entrepreneurs. In 1893, Belfast Chamber of Commerce recited this argument to William Gladstone, the British Prime Minister, writing: 'We were a small, insignificant town in the eighteenth century; since the Union, we have made progress second to none.'

At the same time, Ulster unionism was also rooted in exaggerated fears regarding the likely consequences of Irish self-government. Its supporters assumed that Home Rule would in practice mean 'Rome rule'. They anticipated a state in which the Catholic Church would exercise an all-pervasive political influence and where religious discrimination would be rampant, with themselves excluded from public life, isolated and impotent. Rumours that their property, even their lives, would be at risk were given credence. In addition, they claimed that constitutional change would herald economic ruin from either the incompetence of a future nationalist-controlled government or the calculated imposition of draconian taxation on northern industry by unscrupulous and grasping Dublin ministers.

Despite the striking and repeated electoral success of Home Rule candidates, unionist leaders inclined to the view that Irish nationalism lacked genuine popular support. They attributed its performance at the polls to the effectiveness of self-seeking nationalist leaders, abetted by the Catholic clergy, in exploiting the ignorance and greed of the peasantry in order to attract their votes. Given the strength of their feelings on the issue Ulster Unionists were, as a last resort, prepared to resist Irish self-government with physical force and to press for the partition of Ireland, with the north-east at least remaining under direct Westminster rule.

By the early 1900s, the unionist leaders had succeeded in building up a strong, united movement in Ulster. They found it more difficult to convince the British public that granting Irish home rule would be a political error. During speaking tours to Britain and in publications, they strove to project themselves as reasonable, responsible and respectable politicians and argued that if Ireland were given self-government, it would pose, through its inevitable domino effect, a potent threat to the survival of the British Empire. They were fully aware that their own more deeply-felt religious objections regarding the iniquity of having Protestants ruled by Catholics would have little or no appeal outside the confines of the province itself.

Sectarian Riots

All too often, however, the best efforts of the unionist leadership were compromised by serious and recurrent eruptions of sectarian rioting in Ulster. These made it all too easy for opponents to portray the movement as bigoted and extreme. Belfast, in particular, had a long tradition of 'holy war'; it possessed in Churchill's phrase 'an underworld ... with dark forces of its own'. There were fifteen serious inter-communal clashes in the city between 1813 and 1900. These were, in part, caused by and certainly helped reinforce Belfast's harsh pattern of religious segregation – Catholics living in the Falls Road, Dock and Short Strand districts, Protestants on the Shankill, in Sandy Row and Ballymacarrett. Mutual isolation and ignorance bred violence; it was endemic in these deprived, disease-ridden, working-class ghettos, where health and education provision were woefully inadequate, housing over-crowded and the police force distrusted by both communities. (The city was predominantly Catholic to 1864, and mainly Protestant thereafter.) Though their occupants had so much in common, the narrow streets in these areas became great nurseries of religious intolerance.

An underlying and potent cause of tension was the dramatic growth and mounting confidence of the Catholic community, concentrated in the west of the city. During the nineteenth century, its numbers rose from one-tenth to one-quarter of Belfast's total population. This ongoing trend inevitably stoked up Protestant fears of eventual engulfment, as well as heightening competition for employment in circumstances where unskilled labour was constantly in surplus. It required little to cause the tinder-box to explode in tribal conflict. Six of the fifteen recorded outbreaks of rioting between

1813 and 1900 were caused directly by the Orange Order's annual Twelfth of July demonstrations. Others were triggered off by apparently innocuous political events elsewhere. In 1864, the unveiling of a monument to Daniel O'Connell, 'the Liberator', in central Dublin resulted in eighteen days of civil unrest in Belfast, in the course of which twelve people died. The worst riots of the century coincided with the debate at Westminster on the first Home Rule bill (1886); between June and October, at least thirty-two people lost their lives and over 370 were wounded.

CHAPTER 2

The Unionist Leaders

The unionist movement faced its greatest challenge yet when, in 1912, the British Liberal government, under Herbert Asquith, introduced a Home Rule for Ireland bill at Westminster. It was the third such bill in a quarter-century. The first was introduced in 1886 by Gladstone, the Liberal leader, who became convinced that Irish Home Rule was a duty owed by man to God. The bill split his party and was defeated by a revolt among his own backbenchers. His second, in 1893, passed through the Commons, only to be rejected by the Conservative-dominated House of Lords. Gladstone retired the following year.

Nonetheless, the pressure for Irish self-government was tearing British politics apart and when the Liberals introduced a third bill in 1912 its victory seemed assured since it had the support of both Labour MPs and the nationalists. By then, too, the power of the Lords had been clipped, so that they could merely delay legislation (for up to two years) but could not block it altogether.

The unionist movement was now led by James Craig and Sir Edward Carson. More than anyone else, James Craig was responsible for the fact that the unionists were in a position to defy the British government. He was a genial, immoveable Ulsterman of independent means, who had entered politics in 1906 after military service in the Boer War. The significance of his subsequent contribution lay not in his intellectual ability but in his prodigious organisational skills. His objective throughout was a narrow one, but it had a deep resonance amongst his own adulatory supporters – namely to keep the North within the Union, by any and every means.

Edward Carson, a Dubliner and the most successful lawyer of his generation, had a greater vision. He wished simply, indeed naïvely, to preserve the Union of Britain and Ireland. With an élitist detachment, he felt that this was in the best interests of his fellow countrymen; he was an Irish patriot, but not a nationalist. In 1912, he became Ulster Unionist leader and hoped then to foment northern resistance in order to wreck the Home Rule legislation altogether. He brought flair, class and credibility to the movement. Owing to his undoubted charisma, spell-binding oratory and unyielding image, Carson was all but deified in the province of his adoption.

The two northern leaders complemented each other; the sum was greater than the parts. Their initial response to Asquith's bill was one of uncompromising hostility. They hoped to pressure him into abandoning it altogether despite its substantial Commons majority. Later both came to recognise and accept the inevitability of Irish self-government and pressed instead for a compromise solution based on partition – the North to be excluded from the jurisdiction of any future Dublin government and to continue to be ruled direct from Westminster.

Covenant Day

During 1912, the unionists confined their protest activities mainly to monster rallies and meetings in Ulster. Through these the organisers aimed to mobilise and enthuse their own membership, whilst hopefully preserving its discipline. The rallies were also intended to impress opinion elsewhere in the United Kingdom by highlighting the party's strength, unity and determination; they were complemented by a propaganda campaign in Britain itself, explaining and justifying the unionist position.

Covenant Day, 28 September 1912, was by far the most spectacular and elaborate demonstration. The leadership declared the occasion to be a public holiday and, in an atmosphere of fervent religious devotion, almost 450,000 men and women throughout the province signed 'Ulster's Solemn League and Covenant'. The signatories, some writing in their own blood, pledged 'to stand by one another in defending for ourselves and for our children our cherished position of equal citizenship in the United Kingdom, and in using all means that may be found necessary to defeat the present conspiracy to set up a Home Rule parliament in Ireland.'

Formation of Ulster Volunteer Force

In the background, progressively more ominous measures were being taken by the party's leadership. From mid-1912, covert plans were laid for the formation in the North of a provisional government, to be led by Carson, should Britain attempt to impose all-Ireland institutions. In December, it was agreed to form a paramilitary organisation, the Ulster Volunteer Force (UVF), to be composed of all adult males of military age who had signed the covenant. It was a decision which, in due course, helped to transform the face of Irish politics.

At the time, Craig, in particular, regarded the initiative as fully justified. None of the demonstrations and protests which he had masterminded to date had made any observable impression on the Irish policy of British ministers; the Home Rule bill was continuing to make slow but steady and unamended progress through Westminster. Rank-and-file unionist supporters had for months urged the necessity for more drastic action; they had already begun to drill and train in alarming numbers. The UVF was established as a means of preserving their unity and discipline and of exerting additional pressure on the British government. At the same time, of course, it was a means of preparing for the worst – the use of physical force to resist Irish self-government. By mid-1914, 90,000 men had enlisted province-wide, meeting regularly for instruction and practice in local Orange halls and in the parks and demesnes of sympathetic landowners.

Larne Gun-Running

It soon became apparent that, far from impressing opponents, a force armed mainly with spades and wooden rifles merely invited their ridicule and contempt; this, in turn, sapped the morale of the volunteers themselves. It was, therefore, decided to import arms – 140 tons in all – consisting of 35,000 rifles and five million rounds. The consignment was purchased in Germany, transported circuitously via Denmark and finally unloaded at Larne, a port twenty miles north of Belfast. Most arrived aboard a collier, *The Clydevalley*, on the night of 24-25 April 1914 and was rapidly dispersed, under cover of darkness, to big houses and Orange halls throughout Ulster by several hundred waiting motorised vehicles. It has been claimed that this was the first occasion on which the internal combustion engine was used for a military purpose. The motorcade was on such a scale that some local residents at first imagined that war had been declared and that Ireland was being invaded.

The political impact of these developments was traumatic. Cumulatively, they vastly inflated unionist morale and confidence. At the same time, the position of the British government had been demonstrably weakened. It had stood by impotently, whilst both the law and its own authority had been openly flouted; not a single arrest was made or gun recaptured. In the process, its policy options with regard to Ireland had been significantly narrowed. If it attempted now to impose Home Rule on the North, this would almost certainly result in massive bloodshed.

For their part, Irish nationalists began to sense that they had made a most grave political miscalculation. From the earliest stages of the crisis, they had assumed that the Liberals could be relied on to proceed with the Home Rule bill, intact and as promised, and that its opponents, recognising the futility of opposition, would eventually abandon resistance. By late 1913, both assumptions seemed totally misplaced. By then, even the most moderate, or optimistic, of Home Rule supporters had concluded that they, too, should, as a matter of utmost urgency, form a paramilitary organisation to reinforce their demand for self-government and as a counterweight to the UVF.

In November, recruitment to the Irish Volunteer Force (later known as the Irish Republican Army or IRA) began. By July 1914, its total membership throughout Ireland had reached roughly 180,000. During that month, its leaders also organised an illegal shipment of arms from Germany. It was imported, in broad daylight, through Howth, a port north of Dublin, in a calculated attempt to emulate and surpass the drama and daring of the Larne gun-runners. In the short term at least, the existence of the two forces in Ulster helped to restrain their respective supporters and prevent serious disturbances, despite the deepening political tension.

Tory Support for Unionist Resistance

The overall impact of the unionists' campaign in Britain was enhanced by the consistent encouragement it received from the Conservative Party, even when they were forming the UVF to defy Westminster legislation. Conservative leaders shared a genuine sympathy for the unionist cause; they thought it unjust that almost one million loyal British citizens should be summarily expelled from the Union. They also considered that to provide Ireland with even the limited devolved structures and powers envisaged in Asquith's bill would be a grave act of misgovernment, likely to lead to the disintegration of the Empire and certain to leave Britain more exposed to foreign invasion.

Their response was also partly based on crude political calculation. They were unashamedly and irresponsibly 'playing the Orange card'. Convinced that their support for Ulster's resistance would appeal to the atavistic racial and religious prejudices of the British electorate, especially in England, they hoped to exploit the Irish question to hound the beleaguered Liberals from office. But there was also some evidence of broad popular sympathy in Britain for the unionist position: the issue contributed to a succession of government by-election defeats between 1912 and 1914. During these years, two million people, including Edward Elgar and Rudyard Kipling, signed an anti-Home Rule petition and a British League was formed which claimed that, if required, it could put 10,000 men into the field to help the Ulstermen resist Dublin rule.

The Curragh Mutiny

The unionist movement attracted the sympathy of other vital and elevated elements in British public life. King George V privately sought to persuade Asquith to make concessions to the Ulstermen and warned that he might otherwise either dismiss the Prime Minister from office or refuse to sign the Home Rule bill (a legal requirement if it was to become law). Either course would have broken the spirit of the Constitution and precipitated a major political crisis.

Not surprisingly, given its predominantly privileged background, the officer class in the British army also inclined towards the unionists. With utter disregard for the war-clouds gathering in Europe, the Conservative Party had been considering what legislative means could be used to undermine the discipline of the army, particularly if deployed in Ireland. This proved to be unnecessary; the extent of the bias within its upper ranks was graphically exposed during the Curragh Mutiny.

The Curragh was then Britain's premier military base in Ireland. During the spring of 1914, Sir Arthur Paget, the General Officer Commanding based there, became convinced (mistakenly) that his men would soon be dispatched North to crush the incipient unionist resistance to Home Rule. To establish their likely response, he decided, somewhat foolhardily, to assemble the cavalry officers together on 20 March and offered them a stark but simple choice – either to indicate their willingness to march on Ulster or be dismissed from the service. Fifty-seven of the seventy present opted for dismissal.

Civil War in Ireland

Both the unionist and Conservative leaders, having abandoned their earlier outright opposition to Irish self-government, were by then urging Asquith to adopt a solution based on partition. In any case, the Liberal ministers were themselves coming to regard some such arrangement as a possible basis for compromise. Their sustained record of prevarication and inaction since 1912 had left them few alternatives and the Curragh Mutiny had finally undermined any residual confidence that the British army could be relied upon to repress opposition to Home Rule in Ulster, if required to do so.

To nationalists, constitutional or otherwise, permanent partition was utterly unacceptable. John Redmond, the Home Rule Party leader, stated firmly that his members could not be 'consenting parties to the mutilation of the Irish nation'. In late July 1914, a last-ditch conference held, at George V's suggestion, in Buckingham Palace predictably failed to reach agreement. Bloody civil war seemed unavoidable; Carson fatalistically observed: 'We shall have once more to prove the manhood of our race.'

The outbreak of the conflict in Europe, however, forestalled this prospect, temporarily at least. Carson and Redmond immediately and unreservedly supported Britain's war effort and agreed to postpone the resolution of the Irish question until after hostilities had ceased. With palpable relief and evident surprise, Asquith observed: 'God moves in mysterious ways.' His foreign minister, Sir Edward Grey, whilst noting that 'the lamps [were] going out all over Europe', added that Ireland was now 'the one bright spot'.

Battle of the Somme

In the course of the war, the unionists' position became politically stronger, so increasing the likelihood of an eventual solution based on partition. At the outset, Carson had declared: 'England's difficulty is not Ulster's opportunity, but our difficulty: we shall not purchase terms by selling our patriotism.' A substantial proportion of the UVF's members volunteered for service in the 36th (Ulster) Division, a British army unit, raised specifically for them by Lord Kitchener. In October 1915, it transferred to France. On 1 July 1916 (the date on which the Battle of the Boyne had traditionally been celebrated), it was thrown into the Battle of the Somme. On that fateful day, the British army suffered the largest number of casualties in its history. Within two days, 5,500 men of the 36th were reported dead, wounded or missing. The scale of their sacrifice confirmed, in the words of a recent authority, that 'No British government would ever force Ulster Unionists to accept Dublin rule.' It certainly helped to determine the content of the post-war Irish settlement.

Meanwhile, at Westminster, the ineffectiveness of the Liberal cabinet (exposed pre-war by its mishandling of Irish affairs) led eventually to its being replaced by a Conservative-dominated coalition government. In December 1916, Lloyd George, the 'Welsh wizard', became prime minister. Though a Liberal, he was increasingly dependent during his term of office (which ended in 1922) on the support of Conservative MPs; their opportunities to help unionists increased with their powers.

Government of Ireland Act, 1920

In 1919, British ministers considered the Irish question once more. Their 'solution' was the Government of Ireland Act, 1920. Its terms reflected a broad consensus which had gradually emerged since 1914 between the Conservative and Liberal parties. Ireland was to be partitioned and two Irish parliaments formed – one in Belfast with jurisdiction over the six north-eastern counties ('Northern Ireland'), the second in Dublin with authority over the other twenty-six counties ('southern Ireland'). Each was to be granted limited ('transferred') powers of self-government (similar to those offered repeatedly in the earlier Home Rule bills) over, for example, law and order, policing, transport, education and housing. The major areas of responsibility were 'excepted', (i.e. lay outside their competence) and included matters such as foreign policy, the army, almost all taxation and, of course, the constitutional position of the Crown as Head of State. Decisions on these were retained at Westminster, whose sovereignty over the whole island was to remain undiminished.

'In his heart' Lloyd George hoped that this measure would satisfy moderate opinion throughout Ireland. He considered that previous imperial commitments to the Unionists were being fully honoured by the offer of partition. They had, of course, expected and would have preferred continued direct rule from Westminster for the partitioned area. The British cabinet, however, considered that northern nationalists would resent this more than being governed by their fellow-countrymen in Belfast. In addition, it was anxious to withdraw at last from the day-to-day administration of affairs in Ireland, provided that Britain's vital interests there were adequately protected.

Leading British politicians generally hoped that the two new Irish states would, in due course, unite, whilst remaining closely bound to Britain. To facilitate this process, the 1920 Act made provision for a Council of Ireland. It was to be composed of twenty representatives, elected by each of the Belfast and Dublin parliaments, and was to discuss 'matters of common concern'. As a further inducement to the formation of unitary institutions, Westminster specified a number of additional ('reserved') powers relating to matters such as banking, the post office and the court system; these were to be transferred to a future thirty-two-county Irish government, once this was established.

Ulster Unionist Reaction

Though Unionist MPs abstained from voting on the 1920 Act, they regarded its terms as the most favourable that they were likely to be offered. They quickly came to recognise that a regional parliament, in which they held a majority, would provide them with much greater security than direct rule from Westminster. This was especially the case as they deeply distrusted the rising Labour movement in Britain and were painfully aware that even the Conservative party was now supporting them more as a fulfilment of past pledges than from current conviction.

Rather than resist the legislation, Craig and his colleagues sought to amend it, with a view to copper-fastening their domination of the future Northern Ireland parliament. For example, British ministers favoured placing the whole province of Ulster (all nine counties) under the jurisdiction of the prospective Belfast government. *The Times* of London strongly supported this preference, arguing that the resulting 'strong nationalist minority ... would not merely be a guarantee of the protection of the rights and interests of that minority, and of a certain harmony of development between the two Irish states, but it would also prove a powerful force working in the direction of Union.' Craig, however, pressed successfully for six-county partition. His motives were concisely stated by Walter Long, an earlier unionist leader, who commented: 'The inclusion of Donegal, Cavan and Monaghan would provide such an access of strength to the Roman Catholic party that the supremacy of the Unionists would be seriously threatened.' The resulting partitioned area had a two-thirds Protestant majority: *The Irish Times* predicted that it would result in 'the permanent division of Ireland and ... the maintenance of sectarian strife'.

Nationalists and the 1920 Act

Irish nationalists rejected the 1920 Act. They opposed partition which conflicted with their view of Ireland as an indivisible unitary state, 'a seamless garment'. Also, over the three previous decades, their perceptions had radically changed; they were increasingly drawn towards the goal of an independent, united Irish republic. Westminster's prolonged failure between 1886 and 1914 to pass legislation granting them even limited self-government had caused mounting disillusion and frustration. After 1912, unionist militancy proved contagious; it infected nationalist attitudes, contributing to the decision to form, and later arm, the Irish Volunteers.

In wartime, the Easter Rising (24-29 April 1916) also profoundly influenced majority opinion. The insurgents in Dublin proclaimed an independent republic and with a force of 1,600 men occupied key buildings in the city.

Though their rebellion elicited little public support at the time and was repressed by Crown forces with relative ease, Britain's subsequent decision to execute fifteen of the rebel leaders transformed the atmosphere. It outraged the nationalist population, generated a deep and abiding hatred of Britain and heightened sympathy for the vision of the dead patriots – a thirty-two county republic to be achieved by force. In January 1919, the Irish War of Independence began. The conflict resulted both from the changing aspirations of Irish nationalists and from Britain's persistent unwillingness to offer them more than the limited Home Rule powers first suggested by Gladstone in 1886. The 1920 Act brought no abatement in its intensity. Despite Lloyd George's hopes for it, its enactment at Westminster passed almost unnoticed in nationalist Ireland; its terms were regarded as irrelevant by the entire Irish leadership.

CHAPTER 3

The New State of Northern Ireland

The Government of Ireland Act came into operation on 3 May 1921. Little over a month later, on 22 June, George V inaugurated the Northern Ireland Parliament amidst the grey splendour of Belfast's City Hall. Though provided with limited powers, its members were nonetheless to be responsible for the 'peace, order and good government' of the State. This area was thus separated from the rest of Ireland; partition had begun. Ironically, the first Irish parliament in 120 years had been installed in Belfast, citadel of Ulster unionism which had been founded with the sole purpose of opposing Irish self-government in any form.

The devolved structures established then survived for over fifty years. Though the area remained part of the United Kingdom (sending thirteen MPs to Westminster), it was equipped with a full panoply of institutions of its own, each replicating the British model. It had its own parliament consisting of the King (represented by a Governor from December 1922), a twenty-six seat Senate, a fifty-two member Commons, an executive with seven departments of government and a legal system.

The new state was defined by a meandering and indefensible border, 250 miles long, which enclosed two-thirds of the historic province of Ulster (the six counties of Antrim, Armagh, Down, Fermanagh, Londonderry and Tyrone and the two county boroughs of Londonderry and Belfast, the capital). Its territory of 5,462 square miles comprised roughly one-sixth of the land area of Ireland but its population (of 1.27 million) represented over one-quarter of the total for the whole island. Its title 'Northern Ireland' is geographically misleading since the northernmost part of Ireland, County Donegal, is in what is now the Republic. Nationalists have always preferred to use the term 'Six Counties' rather than the official designation, which they consider implies that Ireland is divisible. However improbably, the phrase 'Six Counties' was first coined by George V when opening the Northern Ireland parliament.

Craig becomes Prime Minister

Sir James Craig became the region's first prime minister. He accepted the position reluctantly and from a sense of duty, mainly because he had to abandon a promising ministerial career at Westminster. He had succeeded Carson as unionist leader in January 1921. Carson himself had no interest in the appointment. He was ill, ageing and had little or no administrative talent. In any case, Ulster had been, for him, a means to an end – the total defeat of Irish Home Rule – and failure to achieve this objective caused him bitter disappointment. It would have been an embarrassment for him to have become the first premier of Northern Ireland. In the end, it provided him with a tomb, but at no time a home.

In retrospect, the first two years were the most formative in the history of the North. At the time of George V's visit, there seemed valid reason to view the future with hope. In his speech, the King had implored both North and South to 'stretch out the hand of forbearance and conciliation, to forgive and forget, and to join in making for the land which they love a new era of peace'. His emotional, personal appeal proved to be the prelude to a truce (effective from 11 July 1921), which was followed over the next six months by delicate and tense negotiations between the British government and the Irish nationalist leadership. Meanwhile, in Belfast, Craig's speeches suggested both a sensitivity to his responsibilities and an awareness of the apparent opportunity to break the mould of sectarian division and conflict which had so long characterised the history of the province.

Craig promised to be 'absolutely fair' in his administration and to 'look to the people as a whole' and he appealed for co-operation and friendship with the Irish nationalist leadership in Dublin. Guided by Westminster, which had retained its full sovereign powers, it seemed possible that a just and stable government might emerge in Northern Ireland, co-existing in harmony with its southern neighbour.

Defects in the 1920 Act

Such hopes proved illusory. In part, the cause lay with the governmental structures established under the 1920 Act. They were devised without regard for the realities of Northern Irish life and the British model on which they were based proved totally unsuited to the region's needs. The Westminster system of simple majority rule provided the foundation for the Unionist Party's absolute monopoly of power throughout the fifty-year lifetime of the post-1921 Belfast parliament. During that entire period not a single Catholic nationalist held Cabinet office.

Also, though religious discrimination by the regional administration was prohibited, in practice the rights of the minority were inadequately protected. There was no bill of rights, the local courts proved incapable of rectifying the grievances of individuals in cases where blatant discrimination had occurred and Westminster had no effective means of supervising the activities of local ministers, short of imposing direct rule. The Northern Ireland government was by and large competent, but far too responsive to pressure from extremist supporters. Its members lacked experience, generosity, vision and, perhaps as important, adequate tax-raising powers. They were therefore unable to implement a coherent legislative programme, relevant to the context of social and economic deprivation within the Six Counties.

The State under Siege

In addition, Craig and his colleagues faced problems which were possibly insoluble and certainly more grave than they had ever imagined likely. The traditional paranoia of Unionist leaders, their 'siege mentality', was massively reinforced during 1921-22, when the Six Counties experienced the reality of siege. The Dublin government, persuaded by Michael Collins (December 1921-August 1922),F refused to recognise the Belfast parliament and used every means available to destabilise and overthrow it. Northern nationalists were shocked and appalled by their sudden transformation into a vulnerable and isolated minority and generally identified with this response. They supported a programme of passive resistance, abstentionism by their elected representatives and, in some cases, the use of physical force.

Craig's difficulties were aggravated by the economic context. From late 1920, deepening recession inevitably fuelled sectarian tension and violence. In Belfast, during July 1921 alone, twenty-six people died and forty were wounded as a result of civil disorder. Earlier, the

War of Independence (January 1919-July 1921) had left a permanent and controversial imprint on security provision locally. IRA activity during the conflict prompted a revival of the UVF. In September 1920, the British government, desperately seeking to restore order in Ireland, recruited its members into an official police force, the Special Constabulary, formed only in Ulster. The decision delighted unionists: they had lobbied for it. The nationalist community were outraged and Joe Devlin, MP for West Belfast, complained angrily that Westminster was 'arming pogromists to murder Catholics'.

The British premier, Lloyd George, offered the beleaguered northern government neither guidance nor support. His priority, after agreeing a truce with the IRA on 11 July 1921, was to reach agreement in his delicate negotiations (July-December 1921) with the southern nationalist leadership. To facilitate this, he exerted powerful pressure on Craig to accept Irish unity and Dublin rule. Also, in order not to strain or prejudice the outcome of the talks, Westminster refused to transfer any actual powers to the Belfast parliament until November 1921. Most galling of all to unionists was the fact that the terms of the truce itself were applied, without consultation, to Northern Ireland. As a consequence, the Special Constabulary was stood down, British army units in the province were virtually confined to barracks and full legal status was conferred on the IRA; it was free to reorganise, recruit, train and drill openly. By the spring of 1922, its estimated strength in the North was 8,500 volunteers. Its political wing, Sinn Féin, was the other chief beneficiary. It became the dominant force in northern nationalism outside Joe Devlin's secure political base in West Belfast.

The Treaty and Northern Ireland

The Anglo-Irish Treaty signed by the British and Irish delegations on 6 December 1921 perpetuated northern insecurity. It offered the twenty-six counties (henceforth the Irish Free State) substantially greater powers than had been available under the 1920 Act but not the fully-fledged republic most nationalists aspired to. Though it did not provide for Irish unity, southern leaders were willing to accept it, partly because they were convinced that its terms would secure eventual unification. Their hopes centred on Article 12 which stated that, if the Belfast parliament refused to accept Dublin rule, the boundaries of Northern Ireland would be revised by a future Boundary Commission. They assumed that the findings of this proposed enquiry would be determined predominantly by the wishes of the northern people themselves on a county-by-county basis; in Collins's phrase: 'majorities must rule'. Accordingly, sweeping boundary changes were anticipated, affecting whole counties, including Fermanagh and Tyrone, in both of which nationalists outvoted unionists. Irish officials calculated that up to 800,000 persons (almost two-thirds of Northern Ireland's population) would eventually be transferred to Dublin's jurisdiction; the residual rump was not expected to be viable.

Inevitably, this section of the Treaty enormously boosted the morale and expectations of the northern minority, especially in border areas. It further encouraged non-recognition of the Belfast parliament and even support for physical force. At the same time, it caused alarm, even panic, amongst Ulster Unionists and confirmed their disillusion with and distrust of the British government.

'The Troubles', 1922

The circumstances of Northern Ireland's birth helped permanently to distort its political structures. Civil unrest (euphemistically referred to as 'the Troubles') was the most immediate problem facing Craig and his colleagues in early 1922. The prolonged political uncertainty as well as mounting unemployment helped foment traditional sectarian hatreds and conflict. In addition, the IRA, revitalised by the truce, renewed its campaign during February, hoping to overthrow the apparently vulnerable Belfast parliament. In Dublin, Collins covertly provided its units with arms and personally advised them on targets and tactics. Like them, he aimed to destabilise and ultimately to absorb the Six Counties. Three meetings with Craig between January and March 1922 had heightened his own personal sense of frustration and exasperation over the partition question. The two leaders had been unable to reach agreement on the critical issue of future boundary revision. Craig would agree only to minor border rectification which Collins considered would cheat nationalists of their legitimate gains and rights under the Treaty.

The deepening split in nationalist Ireland over the terms of the Treaty provided Collins with an additional motivation for intervening in the North. He wished to arrest the drift towards Irish civil war by diverting attention towards, and perhaps ending, the iniquity of the border. He also sought to protect the lives and property of northern nationalists from loyalist attack, since he sincerely doubted the willingness or ability of local security forces to do so. He had already emerged as self-appointed spokesperson for the minority. He frequently raised its treatment in talks with Westminster and encouraged and helped finance its strategy of passive resistance towards Belfast institutions. From February 1922, North-South relations rapidly deteriorated to the point of undeclared war.

Mounting violence and suspicion of southern involvement encouraged a laager mentality amongst unionist ministers. Craig defiantly declared that 'not an inch' of the land area of the Six Counties would be forfeited to the Dublin authorities, whatever the findings of any future Boundary Commission. Recent experience had also instilled in him an equally profound distrust of British ministers. His policy priority was, therefore, to expand the security forces under his government's control and to extend its emergency powers so that, independently of London, it could cope with any disorder short of full-blown cross-border invasion. During the spring of 1922 the number of Special Constables was therefore drastically increased. From February, they bore the main burden of security work, having been reactivated then for the first time since the truce. Meanwhile legislation was prepared to form a new police force, the Royal Ulster Constabulary (RUC) which became operational on 1 June 1922.

The Special Powers Act, 1922

Finally in April, the Civil Authorities (Special Powers) Act became law. It provided the 'civil authority' (the Minister of Home Affairs) with draconian emergency powers – for example, to impose the death penalty for certain firearms and explosives offensives (with flogging and imprisonment for others), to prohibit inquests and to arrest without warrant. It also permitted the Minister, Dawson Bates, to delegate any of these powers to even the lowest-ranking police officer and to make further regulations as required without consulting parliament. The need for some such measure was suggested by the fact that, between 1 January 1922, and 1 March 1922, eighty-three murders had been committed in Belfast, without a single person being brought to justice. Though the legislation was rarely applied, Craig hoped that its existence might reassure and satisfy his own supporters and so reduce the level of sectarian attacks by loyalist gangs on Catholic civilians. His actions stemmed in part from his anxiety to attract the sympathies of the British government which remained, after all, the irreplaceable source of money, troops and ultimately power.

Ministers in Britain observed this succession of security initiatives with the most profound feelings of unease. They were especially alarmed by the expansion of the Special Constabulary. It was by now an almost exclusively Protestant force and had a reputation for ill-discipline. Though constituted, funded and armed by Westminster, it was quite conceivable that its members could be actively deployed against British troops, for example, if Craig's cabinet decided to resist implementation of the Boundary Commission's findings.

Despite their genuine concern, however, Lloyd George and his colleagues rejected the obvious option of using the army itself to preserve order in Belfast or to guard the Northern Ireland border. They feared that this would be interpreted in Dublin as a breach of the truce, which was still technically in operation. It might therefore antagonise Collins and undermine the Treaty settlement. Alternatively, it could well lead to violent clashes with the IRA and these could escalate ultimately into a renewal of the Anglo-Irish war. Furthermore, Britain wished to avoid giving observers any impression that partition was being imposed on Ireland as would inevitably be suggested by the overt use of military force.

The Violence Peaks

In May 1922, both the IRA campaign and the level of sectarian violence peaked. During that month seventy-five persons, fifty-two of them Catholics, were murdered in Belfast. In response, Craig's government fully utilised its emergency powers for the first time. On 22 May, over two hundred republican suspects were interned and held aboard a ship, the *Argenta*, off the Larne coast. Simultaneously, a number of republican movements (including the IRA) was proscribed. Soon afterwards, a curfew was imposed throughout the Six Counties.

Meanwhile, Collins protested vehemently to London, alleging that northern Catholics were the victims of a sectarian pogrom and that the Special Constabulary was implicated. He pleaded with Britain to impose martial law or, at least, hold a full judicial inquiry into the security measures taken by ministers in Belfast. Though neither suggestion was acted upon, Lloyd George was certainly responsive and deeply apprehensive. He expressed privately his concern at his cabinet's recent role in Ulster: 'The first murders were of Catholics ... yet no-one ... was ... punished and no inquiry ... We had armed 48,000 Protestants.'

On 27 May, pro-Treaty IRA units occupied a remote border salient in South Fermanagh, which included the villages of Belleek and Pettigo. After strident appeals from Craig, they were expelled two weeks later by British troops, acting under orders from Churchill, the Colonial Secretary. From early June 1922, the levels of violence in Northern Ireland gradually petered out. This was partly attributable to the far-reaching security measures which had been taken by Craig's government over previous months. It had recruited a police force of roughly 40,000 (Special Constabulary and RUC), one member for every six families living in the Six Counties. During the weeks after 22 May, a total of 728 republican suspects had been interned. Others were subject to exclusion orders. Their supporting organisations were proscribed, a province-wide curfew imposed and most border roads closed.

The outbreak of civil war in the south (which began on 28 June) also contributed directly to the restoration of order in the North. It distracted and finally absorbed the IRA gunmen. Collins, his government struggling to survive, personally instructed all northern units to suspend their activities. They were, in any case, anxious to do so. Their morale was low and they had suffered a crippling haemorrhage of volunteers and arms, either having been withdrawn across the border into the Free State or having been interned. Moreover, they were aware that the minority as a whole had become war-weary.

Mounting indifference to their campaign was evidenced by the improving quality and growing volume of confidential information reaching the security forces from Catholic areas of Belfast. Seamus Woods, an IRA officer commanding northern divisions, conceded that the 'position [was] hopeless', that the national spirit was 'practically dead', and that, if the campaign was to be continued, it would be necessary to 'mete out capital punishment' within their own community in order to restore and preserve its discipline.

Impact of the Troubles on Nationalists

Though this first phase of the Troubles had been brief, it had left the nationalist side exhausted, fatalistic and apathetic. Their casualties had been relatively high. Of 428 persons killed in the two years to 18 June, 1922, two-thirds were of the Catholic minority which formed roughly one-third of the population. It has been estimated that 8,500 were driven from their jobs and 23,000 from their homes and as many as 50,000 may have fled the province altogether. It may not have been the pogrom which Collins and others claimed but the northern nationalists certainly suffered disproportionately.

The experience of those years confirmed many Catholics in their lasting contempt for and hatred of both partition and the northern parliament. Thereafter, they never recognised the State as their own and their sense of alienation was transmitted from one generation to the next. Their hostility was directed especially at the Special Constabulary, which they regarded as sectarian in composition, politically extreme and violently partisan. One provincial paper dismissed its members as 'the dregs of the Orange Lodges, equipped to overawe nationalists.' The unionist leadership was aware of and sought to counteract the disciplinary problems endemic in a mainly part-time force, inadequately trained, virtually unpaid and originally recruited from a paramilitary force, the UVF.

The Northern Ireland government, however, had to place heavy reliance on the Specials. Despite Craig's opposition, the British government had disbanded the all-Ireland regular police force, the Royal Irish Constabulary (RIC), with effect from 31 May 1922 and during the preceding months it had been demoralised and virtually inactive. When its replacement in the Six Counties, the Royal Ulster Constabulary, was established on 1 June, it had only 1,100 members (one-third of its establishment) and was without any adequate system of intelligence. The sixteen battalions of British troops in the North were under Westminster control and by and large confined to barracks for reasons which had little or nothing to do with the security requirements of Northern Ireland.

The Arming of the Protestants

The predominantly Protestant composition of the Special Constabulary and RUC was predictable and probably unavoidable. Potential Catholic recruits were deterred by the likelihood of IRA retribution and by the certainty of social ostracism within their own community. In border areas especially, nationalists retained high hopes that the Boundary Commission would transfer them to southern jurisdiction and it was widely thought that, if they were meanwhile to join the northern security forces, it could only compromise their position at a future enquiry. In any case, most members of the minority opposed partition and had no interest in joining bodies whose primary function was to help enforce it.

In addition, they were further discouraged by the abundant evidence of institutionalised sectarian bias on the part of the Belfast authorities, and not just in the operation of the security forces. For example, the courts dealt more harshly with Catholics than with Protestants charged with similar offences. Also, the government's emergency powers to intern, flog, etc, were applied almost without exception against republican suspects and rarely against unionist paramilitaries or murder gangs. Within its new jurisdiction it failed to preserve the very essence of unionism – British institutions, based on liberal, democratic values and principles.

Other fateful decisions taken by the Belfast government in 1922 had similarly unfortunate long-term consequences. When taking office the previous year, it had inherited seventy-five local authorities. These had been elected under a form of proportional representation (PR), introduced by Westminster in 1919 specifically to ensure that minority groups throughout Ireland had adequate representation. Twenty-four of these bodies (32 percent) were nationalist- or Labour-controlled and many of the former refused from the outset to recognise the northern parliament, pledging their allegiance instead to Dáil Éireann in Dublin.

Initially, in December 1921, Craig and his colleagues had responded to these embarrassing and delicate circumstances by rushing through legislation which enabled them to replace persistently recalcitrant or unco-operative councils temporarily with paid commissioners appointed by themselves. In May 1922, however, they introduced a bill which abolished PR altogether in local government elections and also empowered them to redraw the electoral boundaries. Their crudely political objective was to reduce both the number of non-unionist councillors and the proportion of councils which they controlled and to increase unionist representation. The timing of the measure was related to the approaching Boundary Commission. The prospect of this enquiry made it seem vital for unionists to regain their majorities on, for example, Fermanagh and Tyrone county councils, both in nationalist hands, and on other lesser authorities. Otherwise party members feared the wholesale transfer of large tracts of Northern Ireland to the South.

Six County-ministers were motivated by one other equally pressing consideration. PR had, as Westminster intended, favoured minority parties generally. The Labour party in particular had benefited from its introduction and it was non-committal in its attitude towards partition. The government feared that it might in time attract a substantial section of the Protestant working-class vote and that the Unionist Party might, as a result, lose its majority position in the Belfast parliament. In these circumstances, the Union itself might well be jeopardised.

Michael Collins, on behalf of northern Catholics, protested strongly to London about the bill. He argued that it was not only a blatant attack on their civil rights but also a crude attempt to defraud them of their claim before the Boundary Commission and so to subvert Article 12 of the Treaty and prevent unity. Westminster reacted by delaying the measure but ultimately ratified it. Their restrained, weak response was partly because it was clear that the ministers in Belfast were acting within their transferred powers under the 1920 Act. In addition, the British government hesitated to provoke a constitutional crisis since Craig was threatening resignation if the measure was blocked, followed by an election on the issue. Lloyd George and his cabinet were therefore concerned that they might in the end be left with no option but to impose direct rule on the province, an action which they were desperately seeking to avoid.

Gerrymandering Tactics

After the bill became law, the unionist leaders set about redrawing local government electoral boundaries. A series of public enquiries was held in areas where nationalist and unionist voting strength was roughly even and where any change was, therefore, highly sensitive. Suspecting a wholesale gerrymander and consistent with their strategy of refusing to recognise Northern Ireland institutions, Catholics generally boycotted the hearings. In the few instances where they made submissions, an amicable and fair settlement was reached. In contrast, unionists attended the enquiries in force, equipped with laboriously detailed submissions, most of which were eventually adopted with little or no amendment.

In the subsequent 1924 local elections, Catholics in the fervently nationalist districts of Fermanagh, Tyrone, South Armagh and South Down similarly boycotted the polls, thereby reducing the elections to a farce. After further contests in 1927, the Nationalist and Labour parties controlled just twelve councils (16 percent of the total), exactly half the number they had won in 1920 under proportional representation. In the process, they lost not just majorities and seats but also fair access to the expanding patronage exercised by local authorities – to construct and allocate houses, to offer building contracts and to employ labour.

Despite retaining absolute sovereignty over Northern Ireland, British ministers proved unwilling to exercise it, even when issues of justice and democratic principle were at stake. They had power but refused to accept responsibility. Worst of all, however, the abolition of PR and the adoption of new electoral areas were major acts of misgovernment and an abuse of their power by the unionist leaders themselves. Gerrymandered local authority boundaries, regularly updated by subsequent Belfast governments in response to shifting demographic patterns, became a permanent and infamous feature of the North's electoral landscape. They were among the core grievances which were opposed by the Civil Rights movement forty years later and which helped to topple the Stormont parliament.

The Education Act, 1923

The Catholics' repudiation of the northern state also led to the refusal of their representatives, including members of the hierarchy, to participate in the 1922 enquiry into educational reforms. Over three hundred Catholic Church-owned schools refused either to recognise the Department of Education in Belfast or even to accept payments from it. The Free State authorities facilitated this response and between February and October, 1922, paid the salaries of the teachers in the schools affected, at a cost of £18,000 per month.

Despite its restricted consultation process, the 1923 Education Act represented a rare example of vision on the part of Craig's cabinet. Through it, ministers aimed to establish an efficient, non-sectarian, democratically accountable system, with Protestant and Catholic children educated together, with no provision of religious instruction inside compulsory hours of attendance and with administration becoming the responsibility of committees set up by the local authorities.

The measure was still-born. The Catholic hierarchy adamantly refused to transfer its schools to public control, whilst Protestant clergy agitated ferociously and successfully for legislative amendments which were passed in 1925 and 1930. As a result of these, religious education, known as 'bible instruction', became compulsory in the schools administered by local authorities. Its content was Protestant in nature and, as such, doctrinally unacceptable to the minority. Teachers could be required to teach it and a candidate's religion could be taken into account when management committees were making appointments to school posts. In effect, State schools became Protestant schools, geared to the needs of the majority community. As the local education department met all of their costs, the government was, in practice, endowing the Protestant faith. This was *ultra vires* under the terms of the 1920 Act and, though ministers were so informed by the northern Attorney General, the system remained unreformed until 1947.

The Boundary Commission

The hopes of the Catholic minority that the Boundary Commission would deliver nationalist areas, certainly those near the border, to Dublin's jurisdiction, possibly leaving the North no longer viable, proved to be totally ill-founded. Delayed by the civil war in the Free State and by Craig's prevarication, the enquiry was not initiated until late 1924. When the Commissioners eventually met, they perceived it as their function to suggest only minor border modification. Also, guided by the clear wording of the Treaty (Article 12), their recommendations took into account economic and geographical considerations and not just, as southern leaders would have preferred, the wishes of the people themselves. Had their findings been implemented, the North's long, tortuous border would have been shortened by some fifty miles, some 31,000 persons would have been transferred to the Free State (including those living in such recurrent trouble spots as Crossmaglen in South Armagh) and 7,500 from the south to Northern Ireland.

Though, arguably, this arrangement was not unreasonable, it was set aside. Since early 1922, Craig's position had been that 'not an inch' of Northern Ireland should be given to the Free State. In 1924, he had made it clear that if the boundary report was unacceptable, he would resign and he warned of a possible violent upheaval in Ulster. In Dublin, Prime Minister WT Cosgrave was equally determined that southern Ireland should lose none of its territory. He was also anxious to foster friendship with the North, believing that this approach would draw it into unity more quickly than Collins's covert attempts to destabilise it. Westminster's sole concern was that the issue should at last be resolved as speedily, peacefully and amicably as possible. On 3 December 1925, an agreement was reached between the three governments, leaving the border unchanged. Churchill remarked that this 'out of court' settlement would be welcomed 'over the whole area of the Empire' as having 'brought peace'. Likewise, Craig was delighted and Cosgrave described it as a 'damned good bargain'. In contrast, northern nationalists felt betrayed, isolated and resentful and looked increasingly to Éamon de Valera, one of the leaders of the 1916 Rising, who had subsequently opposed the Treaty, to champion their cause.

CHAPTER 4

Catholic v Protestant

Between 1925 and 1939, Northern Ireland underwent no fundamental change. It had always been the most politically divided area in the United Kingdom; by the end of this period, it had become the most economically and socially disadvantaged as well. Despite this, Westminster treated it less generously than regions in Great Britain.

Nor did North-South relations improve after the boundary agreement; rather they became embedded in a sterile state of 'cold war'. The persistent refusal of the Dublin government officially to recognise the Six Counties was a significant causal factor. Despite his declining faculties, Craig continued to serve as northern premier until his death in October 1940. In fact, death or ill-health were virtually the only reasons for cabinet change; just twelve ministers were appointed between 1921 and 1939.

The members of the government were, typically, upper-class, conservative in outlook and identified with the majority population. Most (fifty-one out of the fifty-four appointed between 1921 and 1969), belonged to the Orange Order; so did roughly two-thirds of adult Protestant males in the Six Counties. The Order exerted a powerful negative influence on local politics, above all helping to ensure that the Unionist Party remained an exclusively Protestant organisation.

The Northern Ireland parliament was amateurish, ill-informed and docile and had, during its entire fifty year history, a substantial unionist majority. The local civil service was industrious and competent but could exert only limited influence on the more sensitive aspects of government policy (security, representation, etc.). The major constraint on Craig and his colleagues was their administration's lack of financial resources, due to inadequate fiscal powers. This severely narrowed their policy options. It dimmed any prospects they may have had of reviving the local economy, lessened the likelihood of attracting nationalist support and increased the pressure to reward supporters by discrimination in their favour where possible.

Keeping up with Britain

Some of the policies adopted by the government from the early 1920s compounded its financial difficulties, in particular, its decision to introduce into the Six Counties the same unemployment and health insurance, national assistance and pension schemes as were provided by Westminster. Despite their deeply conservative instincts, most ministers considered they had little choice but to follow Britain's lead 'step by step'. This was partly because of fears that to do otherwise might cause working-class unionists to defect *en masse* to the socialists or even to emigrate. There was, also, a widely-held opinion that, as citizens in the North paid taxation at the same levels as elsewhere in the United Kingdom, they should enjoy equivalent social services. The British government itself sympathised with this view and was therefore willing from the mid-1920s to contribute towards their higher relative costs in Northern Ireland.

Nonetheless, some leading local politicians and officials considered that this approach was seriously flawed. They noted that wage levels and the cost of living in the region were substantially lower than in

Great Britain, while it had a significantly higher incidence of poverty and distress. They argued that the limited financial resources available would, therefore, be better spent in responding to the specific needs and circumstances which the government faced rather than in the slavish imitation of Westminster.

Certainly adoption of this expensive policy had unfortunate consequences; vital services such as health, education and housing suffered from underfunding and neglect. As a result, maternal death rates in Northern Ireland actually rose (by 20 percent) in the interwar years, its education provision fell a generation or more behind most of England and Wales and, in 1944, a departmental enquiry estimated that almost one-third of its housing stock was in urgent need of replacement.

Financial considerations, as well as sustained pressure from Westminster, also led to modest cuts in security expenditure during the 1920s. Ministers were encouraged to act by the low level of violence after June 1922. In 1931, James Andrews, the Lord Chief Justice, felt justified in describing Northern Ireland as 'one of the most law-abiding areas of the Empire'.

During the following year, however, political and social tension, caused by deepening economic depressions, became acute throughout the western world. By September 1932, 80,000 workers were unemployed in Belfast. Of these, one-quarter had exhausted their claim to state benefit and had to seek relief from the City's penny-pinching Board of Guardians. The Board offered support at substantially lower levels than were available in comparable urban areas in Great Britain. A report produced by the Presbyterian Church described its grants as inadequate to provide the barest necessities of life. This was a recipe for violence but few could have predicted that it would result in the most impressive demonstration of working-class solidarity in Belfast's history.

Riots of 1932

The Catholics on the Falls and Protestants on the Shankill literally look into each others' backyards. Outsiders have constantly been struck not by their differences but by how much they have in common – non-existent social amenities, exploitative employers, decaying housing, emigrating children. In the autumn of 1932, united momentarily by shared grievances, they made common cause and vented their combined anger against those whom they saw as their oppressors.

A series of public meetings and marches in protest at the niggardliness of the city's relief measures culminated in a mass rally, planned for 11 October. On that day, dense crowds merged on five assembly points, in open defiance of a government ban. In East Belfast the police unwisely attempted to disperse the converging throng with baton charges. Their action provided the catalyst for an eruption of rioting and looting which spread rapidly to the lower Falls and Shankill. Two people died, one Catholic and one Protestant and over thirty were injured.

In alarm, the authorities retreated. Payments to the unemployed were promptly raised and the Guardians' responsibility for supporting the needy was transferred to central government. During the following months ministers sought to cosset and reassure their erstwhile loyalist supporters. Craig quoted from a statement by Jimmy Thomas, Britain's Colonial Secretary, stating that there would be no constitutional change regarding Northern Ireland without the full consent of Stormont (the Belfast parliament). In 1933, the Special Powers

Act, hitherto subject to parliamentary renewal, was made permanent.

Sectarian Tension Grows

Inherited prejudice and whipped-up fears rapidly overwhelmed the shallow roots of inter-communal unity. Sectarian tension, fuelled by persistent economic recession, simmered through the early 1930s, resulting in occasional, generally minor, acts of violence. Feelings were aggravated further in 1935 by unionist celebration of George V's Jubilee. In consequence, on 18 June the government prohibited the annual Twelfth of July demonstrations throughout the Six Counties. Fatefully, it then capitulated and withdrew the ban in the face of openly defiant statements by the Orange Order. With Craig on holiday, the decision was taken by ministers more responsive to loyalist pressures.

As so often in the recent past, the ritual march rekindled 'holy war'. A trivial incident along the Orangemen's route in Belfast's Dock area provided the spark for spontaneous rioting, the worst since 1922, and it instantly spread to the traditional theatres of conflict – the Shankill and the Falls. Within three weeks, eleven people had died (most of them Protestant), 574 were injured, (mostly Catholic) and over 300 families (also mostly Catholic) were driven from their homes. In the opinion of Belfast's coroner, the poor people involved in the violence had been inflamed by the speeches of men in high and responsible positions.

Order was not restored until late August after troops saturated disturbed areas, imposing a curfew and creating a temporary 'peace line' to keep the warring factions apart. Yet the scale and frequency of intercommunal violence and rioting in the North might easily be exaggerated. The eruptions of 1932 and 1935 were exceptional. These years apart, between 1922 and 1950, no more than two to three murders occurred on average per annum; in England and Wales, with thirty times Northern Ireland's population, the comparable figure was 150.

If in 'normal' years, the Six Counties was relatively peaceful, its deepening sectarian divisions certainly distinguished it from other regions in the United Kingdom. After 1922, it became a more exclusively Protestant state. In that year, 400 of the first 1,100 policemen to enrol in the RUC were Catholic, a figure inflated by the significant number recruited from the disbanded RIC. The proportion has fallen steadily since; by 1924 it had dropped to 19 percent and, by 1936, to 17 percent. Likewise, just 10 percent of the Northern Ireland civil service was Catholic in 1934, and for administrative grades a mere 5.8 percent by 1943. Between 1921 and 1972, just two Catholics (Bonepart Wise and Patrick Shea) reached the highest rank of permanent secretary. Ministers did not encourage minority recruitment to the public services; neither they nor the Unionist Party fully trusted its members in responsible positions. The under-representation of Catholics was also because many did not accept the legitimacy of the Belfast parliament, refused to serve it and ostracised those who did. Shea noted the reaction within his own community to his becoming a government official: 'We had joined the enemy ... [we] were lost souls.'

Nationalist MPs enter Parliament

The prospect of a stable, regional democracy emerging in Northern Ireland improved dramatically when, for the first time, Nationalist MPs began to take their seats in the northern Commons from 1925. Over the next two to three years, they strove energetically to construct a strong, political party, called the 'League of the North', with branches throughout the Six Counties. These steps were taken mainly because their previous strategy of non-recognition had proved counter-productive. Between 1921 and 1923 major legislation had been passed in their absence, without their interests being adequately defended or taken sufficiently into account. In the mid-1920s, the *Irish News*, the North's leading nationalist newspaper, wrote of 'the rights [Catholics] chose to sacrifice', through abstention and urged a change of policy. The inter-governmental boundary agreement (December 1925) provided an additional argument for entering parliament. Its terms extinguished residual minority hopes of speedy deliverance to Dublin rule; it was clear that partition would continue for the foreseeable future.

The 'League' never fulfilled its founders' hopes. It came mainly to represent the Catholic Church and its middle-class adherents. Republicans regarded it with disdain, denouncing any recognition of northern institutions. Also, political events since 1920 had traumatised northern Catholics generally – lowering their morale, generating feelings of apathy and alienation – and this adversely affected recruitment to the new party.

Inside parliament, the Nationalist MPs made little impact. They restricted themselves mainly to ritual denunciations of partition and of the government and attempted to disrupt the dull and demure proceedings of the House. Craig brusquely brushed aside their positive proposals on security, representations, etc. He considered that they had, through abstention, denied themselves the opportunity to influence reforms already passed. In any case, he regarded their suggestions as fatally flawed and suspect because their avowed objective was Irish unity rather than the improvement of Northern Ireland. They refused throughout to act as an official opposition though they formed the second biggest party in the Commons.

Meanwhile, the flow of insensitive, even repressive, government legislation continued unabated. League representatives were powerless to prevent either the Special Powers Act from being made permanent or the enactment of successive educational amendments strengthening further the Protestant nature of state-provided schools.

In 1929, the nationalists could offer only verbal protests when PR was abolished in Northern Ireland parliamentary elections. They were not consulted at any time about the content of this controversial measure and their pleas of opposition during Commons debates were utterly ignored. Their leader, Joe Devlin, accurately summarised Craig's intentions: '[He] wants to weaken us ... but it is to wipe out what are called the Labour and independent members.'

The Prime Minister's primary aim was indeed to reduce the parliamentary representation of and support for these smaller political groupings. He perceived them as a threat to the unionist majority in the House and potentially, therefore, to the Union itself. As far as possible, he wished to reduce election contests to a straight fight, unionism versus nationalism, which the former with its built-in majority was bound to win overall. The measure reflected both his siege mentality and lack of vision. Despite passionate appeals from Nationalist MPs and others, British ministers refused to intervene, even to delay the bill. They justified their inaction on the strictly legal grounds that the northern government was acting within its 'transferred' powers under the 1920 Act.

During these years, unionist leaders frequently protested their commitment to liberal principles and values and painstakingly replicated Westminster's procedures in Belfast. In November 1932, they took great pride in the opening of grandiose new parliamentary buildings at Stormont. Behind this imposing facade, however, British standards of democracy were constantly sacrificed in pursuit of the party's priority, the preservation of the Six Counties. When there was a choice between, for example, more stringent security measures and greater respect for the rights of the individual, security considerations triumphed.

Craig, more than any other individual, was responsible not only for the formation of Northern Ireland but also for its ultimate political collapse. After 1922, he entirely failed to devise any long-term strategy. His response to the complex, possibly insoluble, problems he faced, was to let things drift. In particular, he made no sustained attempt to correct the patent injustice and imbalance in the North's institutions and structures resulting from the minority's opting out before 1925. Exhausted by the demands of the pre-partition period and by deteriorating health, it was apparently enough for him that the border, his government and a dominant and united Unionist Party should survive intact.

Dispirited by many years of barren opposition and the refusal of unionists to share power in any form, Nationalist MPs collectively withdrew from the Belfast parliament in 1932, initially for a period of eighteen months. Thereafter, until the end of the Second World War, just two of them took their seats on a regular basis. Their non-attendance was mainly a symptom of disillusionment, impotence and apathy. Unlike their political heirs in the 1960s, they made no attempt to mount a popular, civil rights-style campaign on issues such as gerrymandering or discrimination. Instead, they looked increasingly to de Valera, who led the Fianna Fáil government in Dublin from 1932 to 1948, to draw the attention of British ministers and others to the treatment of northern Catholics.

The Catholic Church in the North

Meanwhile, the Catholic Church in the Six Counties flourished. It was the indirect and enduring beneficiary of the retreat from regional politics by many of its adherents and of their alienation or exclusion from much of public life. It provided a sense of security, instilled confidence and offered a social outlet. It also fostered an all-Ireland perspective and an attitude of non-co-operation towards the Northern Ireland government.

Protestants, therefore, identified it with Irish nationalism and with hostility towards the northern state. They cited these associations to justify discrimination against its members. They tended to exaggerate both its monolithic unity and its political influence. It had, of course, played a central role in the formation of the 'League of the North'. Cahir Healy, one of the League's founders, had stated at the outset that to 'make ... [the party] ... a success, the assistance of the clergy is essential'.

But the hierarchy inevitably mirrored the divisions within the northern minority. Even in 1921, some bishops had favoured Nationalist MPs recognising the Belfast parliament and defending the Church's vital interests there. Others had fervently opposed, fearing that this would prejudice the prospects of Irish unity in the longer term. Cardinal Joseph MacRory of Armagh stated that he was against 'any reconciliation between the Orange party and the Catholics'. During the early 1920s, probably most Catholic clergy became as disillusioned politically as many in their congregations and were just as uncertain as to the wisest course to adopt.

Overall, a sort of dualistic society gradually emerged in the Six Counties after 1921, with Protestants and Catholics inhabiting the same part of the island together but living totally separate and segregated lives. Each community had its own churches, schools, teacher-training colleges, housing estates, public-houses, newspapers, recreational pursuits and, of course, political parties and aspirations. Inter-marriage was rare, especially in rural areas. The northern government generally made no attempt to interfere in the affairs of the minority – by imposing censorship, restricting expression of opinion, interfering with the teaching of Irish in schools or regulating its social organisations and activities.

This relative liberalism in the private sphere was matched by an acute concern amongst ministers to ensure that the public life of Northern Ireland was unionist, Protestant and pro-British in tone and content. They resisted any intrusion of 'Irish' culture and society into the State. For example, the BBC locally was closely monitored for any acceptance of the cultural interests of the nationalist community, any blurring of the distinction between 'Ulster' and 'Ireland'. There was unease at the broadcasting of Catholic church services or of Irish traditional music. The transmission of Gaelic Athletic Association results in 1934 led to such strong protests from unionists that the reports were banned until 1946. The view was widely held amongst party members that they had as much right as nationalists to a state of their own on the island of Ireland. When Craig infamously stated in 1934: 'All I boast is that we are a Protestant parliament and a Protestant state,' he justified his remark by adding: 'Remember in the Free State, they boasted of a Catholic state.'

The Labour Movement

For other northern minorities also the inter-war period was one of frustration and disillusionment. A substantial socialist challenge to unionism might reasonably have been expected. Belfast and the Lagan Valley especially had a substantial working class; James Connolly and James Larkin had been amongst the first to attempt to organise it during the decades before the Great War. The region's basic industries – shipbuilding and textiles – were in irremediable decline after 1920 and the need for social reform was patent. Yet the Labour movement's electoral performance was consistently poor, failing to establish a single safe parliamentary seat either at Westminster or Stormont. It suffered throughout from a lack of competent leadership. Its most able figures quarrelled and some seceded from the party altogether. The Catholic hierarchy's condemnation of socialism as incompatible with church teaching stifled its appeal. The abolition of PR in council and local parliamentary elections in itself reduced the representation and morale of all minority groupings, as the government had intended. Also, the unionist cabinet constantly preempted the demands of the left by keeping local social benefits in line with Britain, 'step by step'. At the same time, its constant manipulation of constitutional issues repeatedly divided the electorate and distracted it from 'real' economic and social issues. As a consequence of these factors, local ministers could legitimately boast

that Protestant industrial workers were 'as strong unionists as you or I'.

Loyalist Sentiment Increases

Whatever the disappointments and disabilities experienced by religious and political minorities between
1921 and 1939, amongst unionists there was a detect-
able growth in regional pride, patriotism, loyalty. A
strong sense of community had already emerged within
the movement before 1914 and this was reinforced by
the survival of the State despite 'the Troubles' of the
early 1920s. Gradually thereafter the Northern Ireland
parliament put down deeper roots; this was largely
Craig's achievement. Carson was ill-at-ease with the
notion of partition. In 1917-1918, he had alienated
supporters in Ulster by making proposals for institutions which he hoped would reconcile them to Dublin
rule and acceptance of an all-Ireland Home Rule parliament.

In contrast, Craig viewed partition with enthusiasm;
he utterly opposed unity. Nonetheless, unlike his cabinet colleagues, he could contemplate the prospect. He
believed it possible that he himself might one day be
persuaded of its merits. In such circumstances he
informed Collins in January 1922 he would 'frankly tell'
the Ulster people that unification was in their interests
and retire from politics. He added that for the present,
such an 'eventuality ... [was] out of the question'.

North-South Relations

Subsequently after 1921, unionist unity and patriotic
feeling were stimulated by the North's persistently
strained relations with the Free State. Belfast ministers

constantly sought to draw favourable comparisons between their own performance and developments across the border. Plans for co-operation between the two states devised at the time of the boundary agreement (December 1925) were never implemented. At that time, Craig and Cosgrave had committed themselves to meet regularly for discussions on matters of common concern; in fact, there was no personal contact whatever between the respective heads of government for the next forty years.

From its inception, Ulster Unionism had been rooted in a fear of engulfment by the nationalist majority in Ireland; this fear proved to be enduring. After partition, its members still viewed the Dublin leadership with what was described by a British politician as 'fundamental distrust'. They were aware of its attempts to destabilise the North during 1920-22 and resented its persistent unwillingness officially to recognise the Belfast parliament. They noted with alarm and took at face value occasional rhetorical outbursts by southern politicians threatening force to achieve unity. Their unease was compounded by the irresistible political rise of Éamon de Valera. He had led the minority who opposed the Treaty (6 December 1921) because of its failure to do the 'fundamental thing' – make Ireland an independent, united republic – and had helped rally the anti-Treaty forces during the Irish civil war. Subsequently he founded the Fianna Fáil party (Soldiers of Destiny) and led it to five successive general election victories, the first in February 1932. Immediately on taking office, he lifted the ban on the IRA within the twenty-six counties and released all Republican prisoners. He then took steps to abolish the oath of allegiance taken to the British crown by southern public servants, so, as it seemed to unionists, opening up these posts to the most politically extreme.

The 1937 Constitution

Five years later, in 1937, de Valera introduced a new Constitution – his most enduring and problematical legacy to Irish society. It was in essence republican and represented the culmination of his fifteen-year campaign against the Treaty. It contained two clauses which rankled with the unionist leadership, both because of their content and the justification which they allegedly gave to subsequent IRA campaigns. Article 2 claimed for the Dublin government jurisdiction over the entire thirty-two counties, stating that 'the national territory consists of the whole island of Ireland'. Article 3 accepted that, in practice, the laws of the State could be exercised only within the twenty-six southern counties 'pending the reintegration of the national territory'.

Although seen in the South at the time as quite divisive, these articles have since become absorbed into the political culture of the State. Taken together, they came to express a very real commitment to Irish unity, if not the means to achieve it, and to reinforce the assertion that all those who live on the island of Ireland are, in effect, Irish citizens. The popular interpretation of them was then, and is still today, that they express a constitutional and territorial claim over Northern Ireland. De Valera was dismissive of northern unionism's insistence on its right to remain apart from the Free State. The two clauses heightened Craig's suspicion of the South; he regarded them as 'very objectionable'. Nonetheless, he responded to them more calmly than most of his supporters, stating that he thought 'it would be a mistake to take too much notice of them'.

Even by virtue of its existence, the Free State exercised a profound influence on the political life of the Six Counties during the inter-war years. The northern minority looked to Dublin for leadership and protection throughout. More than anything else, the alleged cross-border threat helped cement unionist unity. Craig exploited it at successive elections to distract attention from 'real' social and economic issues, so debasing the level of political debate. He and his colleagues also used it to justify, for example, the abolition of PR and the maintenance of inflated security forces and powers. Their concern about the South even influenced the content of Northern Ireland's social legislation. Its pension, unemployment insurance and national assistance schemes were distinguished from those operating in Britain mainly by the inclusion of a residence qualification. This was introduced because of unionist fears of 'peaceful penetration' of the Six Counties by southern citizens. It was thought that they might cross the border in large numbers, aiming ultimately to overturn the pro-Union majority, in the meantime taking advantage of the local system of welfare benefits.

The Widening Gulf

Meanwhile, a gulf gradually widened between the two Irish states during the years after partition. It was both economic and cultural in character. In 1920, unionists in Cavan, Monaghan and Donegal had opposed six-county partition partly on the grounds that Ulster was a geographical and commercial, as well as historical, entity. One of their leaders stated: 'All our trade, business and railways are connected with it.' In 1925, Cosgrave justified the Boundary Agreement, saying that any further change would bankrupt Donegal and force 'thousands of unwilling persons to transfer'.

In fact, the land boundary initially caused only limited damage to cross-border commerce. The flow of goods between North and South had never been strong and Derry's links with Donegal, for example, continued more or less as before until the early 1930s. After 1932, however, officially recorded trade shrank as de Valera transformed the Free State into one of the most protected countries in the world. As a consequence, northern goods were either excluded from or overpriced in southern markets. But, as prices in the respective jurisdictions diverged, the growth of an extensive smuggling trade mitigated the worst effects both of partition and protectionism.

Culturally too the erstwhile border had become ever more like a frontier by 1939. Within the Six Counties, the power and privileges of the Protestant majority became more deeply entrenched. Unionists remained anxious to cooperate with Westminster. They never lost their instinctive loyalty to the Crown, pride in Empire or support for the Union, however much their own internal institutions, standards and values might digress in practice from the much-vaunted British model.

Simultaneously, the South became a more overtly Catholic, Gaelic and republican state, steadily dissolving its links with Britain and, in the process, loosening the bonds which held the Empire itself together. De Valera, in particular, refused to dilute his government's programme and emphasis in order to accelerate unity. He stated that he 'would not tomorrow, for the sake of a united Ireland, give up the policy of trying to make this a really Irish Ireland, not by any means.' 'Time,' he believed, 'would settle the other thing' (i.e. partition).

But as time passed, Ireland's divisions were visibly deepening. Unionists were bound to feel alienated by the 'special position' accorded to the Catholic Church under the 1937 Constitution, by its control of education and its broader moral influence, reflected in the repression of birth control, outlawing of divorce and censorship of literature and films. They interpreted the decline in the southern Protestant population after 1922 as evidence of cultural oppression by the Free State government. They regarded attempts to promote the Irish language in the twenty-six counties as draconian and obscurantist.

As the Dublin authorities severed their links with the Empire, there was a proportionate rise in unionist apprehension with regard to unity. Irish neutrality during the Second World War was viewed from across the border not just as a potent assertion of Irish sovereignty but also as a rejection of British identity, even of the northern majority itself; it did more than anything else to reinforce partition.

CHAPTER 5

Pleasantest Place in Europe

The Second World War was a turning point in Northern Ireland's history. The conflict was the source of much warmer relations between Stormont and Westminster and this provided the basis for the North's best years – the 1950s and early 1960s. These developments could not easily have been foreseen in 1939. On 4 September, Craig affirmed in the Commons that there would be 'no slackening in [Ulster's] loyalty' and that all of its 're-sources' would be placed at Britain's command. Yet, in stark contrast to elsewhere in the United Kingdom, the pace of life locally continued much as before. Of course, rationing, censorship, identity cards and travel restrictions were introduced. But there was no conscription, food was relatively plentiful and, until early 1941, unemployment remained high and no bombs fell. A diarist living in the North described it with justification as 'probably the pleasantest place in Europe'.

Other visitors to the North made less flattering comments. In mid-1942, an informed observer from Great Britain expressed shock at the different, more casual, atmosphere he found in Belfast, specifically – people sunbathing on the lawns in front of the City Hall, being late for appointments, sleeping in the backs of cars. He suggested that if they were to behave like this in London or Liverpool, they would at once be notice-able and might even cause a riot.

The lack of a sense of war was also evident in ways which were less visually obvious. These included the consistently modest level of local voluntary recruitment to the armed forces, recurrent and disruptive labour disputes, initially poor productivity in the major munitions firms (Short & Harland, Harland & Wolff) and widespread apathy towards civil defence (the wearing of gas masks, implementation of blackout regulations, enrolment as wardens, etc). Some ministers acknowledged openly and regretfully that the Six Counties were 'only half in the war'.

Craig's Weak Leadership

Many factors account for this contrast with Britain, such as Northern Ireland's remoteness from the theatre of war and from Westminster, its deep and unique sectarian divisions and the absence of conscription which helped so much to sharpen public attitudes elsewhere. A further reason was the complacency and ineffectiveness of the leadership at Stormont. Craig was the main source of weakness. Ill-health and exhaustion had dogged his efforts after 1921-2. By 1938, a leading local official described him as 'too unwell to carry on'; he was then incapable of more than an hour's work per day and remained in office out of financial necessity and to satisfy the social ambitions of his wife. He led his ageing cabinet (average age sixty-two years, in 1938) in increasingly whimsical and dictatorial fashion and defied growing party pressures to appoint younger men. Though an effective organiser, he lacked true leadership qualities – charisma and, above all, the capacity to develop and implement policies directed towards Northern Ireland's long-term stability and survival. Rather he allowed urgent matters to drift. The incompetence of his government was more difficult to defend or conceal in the context of war. This was especially so after successive Allied military defeats and the formation of a new and dynamic administration at

Westminster, led by Churchill. In 1940, Wilfred Spender, the head of the regional civil service, was therefore convinced that Stormont's ineptitude would finally compel the British government to displace it and impose martial law.

The rapid expansion of Northern Ireland's tillage acreage provided a rare wartime success for the unionist leadership. The total area under the plough rose from 471,000 to 829,000 acres between 1939 and 1942, a greater proportionate increase than was achieved in any other region of the United Kingdom. This apart, ministers displayed their customary zeal in security matters. The internment of IRA suspects began on the first night of the war. The Special Constabulary mounted border patrols and later, in May 1940, provided the nucleus for the newly-formed home guard (the 'Local Defence Volunteers'); it was considered that the policy of open enrolment adopted in Great Britain would merely facilitate republican infiltration of the force. Government-organised recruitment drives to boost the disappointing level of military enlistment met with little or no success. This was possibly in part because local folk memory of the carnage at the Somme in 1916 ran so deep.

In mid-1940, the precautions taken against terrorism and invasion were entirely overshadowed by a threat which seemed far more serious and certainly proved more divisive for the cabinet. Anglo-Irish trade negotiations were then being conducted in London, against the depressing backdrop of Dunkirk and the fall of France; in Churchill's phrase, Britain faced 'the abyss of a new dark age'. At Stormont, it was justifiably feared that constitutional issues would be raised and possibly a deal struck in which de Valera would offer to abandon Irish neutrality in exchange for the ending of partition.

Undoubtedly, some British ministers and military advisers, desperate to gain access to southern ports, would have favoured such an arrangement.

The whole question raised a potentially grave clash of interests between Westminster and Stormont as well as a deep conflict of loyalty within Northern Ireland. After attending initial discussions in London with imperial ministers, Craig was summoned to engage in talks with the southern leader on effective measures for Ireland's defence. He adamantly refused to participate until the Free State entered the war and, in any circumstances, if Irish unity was to be raised. Surprisingly, perhaps, this response was not supported unanimously by his ministerial colleagues. Two of them, Basil Brooke and John MacDermott, would have accepted a change in Northern Ireland's constitutional status had Éire reciprocated by dropping its policy of neutrality and joining in the Allied war effort. For them, the defeat of the Axis powers and loyalty to King and Empire were greater priorities than the preservation of the Six Counties within the Union. To their profound relief, the moment passed without the issue being put to the test; de Valera was resolutely determined to keep the Free State out of the conflict.

On 24 November 1940, Craig died; his last Commons speech four weeks earlier had been a typical, tub-thumping assault on the notion of Irish unity. He was succeeded by his most experienced minister Johnny Andrews; it was an appointment greeted even within his own party with resignation rather than enthusiasm. He was a staid, Ulster linen manufacturer, who for the previous five years had shouldered the heaviest burden of governmental administration at Stormont.

Unwisely, he appointed just one new minister, retaining all of his predecessor's decrepit cabinet, the 'old guard'. He was himself almost seventy years old, his health was deteriorating and he was personally unsuited to wartime leadership. Under his premiership, the Northern Ireland government plumbed new depths of incompetence, as well as progressively losing touch with the changing mood of the electorate.

The Belfast Blitz

The Andrews administration began inauspiciously; in March 1941, it lost its first by-election. (It was in Craig's old seat, North Down; he had represented the county since 1906 and the constituency, unopposed, since 1921.) German air-raids on Belfast followed almost immediately, during April-May. John MacDermott, the minister responsible for civil defence, described it at the time as the least well-protected major city in the United Kingdom. This was partly due to the lethargy of the Stormont cabinet which until late 1940 had assumed that Northern Ireland would not be attacked. The civilian population was both physically and psychologically unprepared for the blitz. Over the course of four bombardments, lasting ten hours in all, 1,100 people died, 56,000 houses in Belfast were damaged (one half of the city's total stock) and £20 million damage, at war values, was caused to property. Belfast came twelfth in the league table of urban areas attacked in the United Kingdom, as measured by the weight of bombs dropped.

During the two worst raids (15-16 April, 4-5 May) mortuaries were over-run and public baths and a large fruit market had to be taken over to cope with Belfast's dead. On both occasions help in fighting fires and in rescue work was requested from all over Northern Ireland, from Britain and from southern Ireland, which thereby risked compromising its policy of neutrality and becoming a target itself. Civilian morale in Belfast all but collapsed. By late May, one official estimated that as many as 220,000 had temporarily fled from the city and had scattered throughout Ulster and beyond. Thousands of others 'ditched'; during the hours of darkness they left the congested and vulnerable working-class terraces and streamed along the main arterial roads to the suburbs to shelter in parks, ditches and hedgerows until first light, when they thought it safe to return home. One cabinet member expressed the opinion that popular anger at the lack of governmental preparation for Luftwaffe attack would result in attacks by irate mobs on Stormont buildings.

Conscription is Rejected

The blitz prompted calls for the government to introduce conscription. Lord Abercorn, the governor, advised Andrews to 'strike when people's feelings were hot'. Initially the prime minister was also enthusiastic. To some of his colleagues this seemed the only possible way to restore civilian discipline and to achieve 'equality of sacrifice'; levels of voluntary enlistment were still modest and even the civil defence services had difficulty recruiting personnel in some areas.

Opinion at Westminster was also favourable to the proposal, as an estimated 50,000 recruits could be raised. But subsequently when it was made public, well-attended protest rallies, organised by nationalist leaders and supported by the Catholic hierarchy, convinced Andrews that its implementation would provoke widespread violence and resistance. He informed British ministers of his reservations and asked them if conscription would really be 'for the good of the

Empire'. Next day, an official statement was issued in London, indicating that conscription would not be extended to Northern Ireland as it would be more trouble than it was worth. A year later, Churchill again advocated conscription when virtually all of Belfast's munitions workers walked out but Andrews again dismissed the suggestion as 'impracticable'.

Brooke becomes Prime Minister

By the winter of 1942-3, there was a broad consensus amongst backbenchers, junior ministers, leading civil servants and party officials that a complete change of leadership was urgently required. Otherwise, it seemed likely that law and order and party unity might collapse and possible that democracy and the Union itself might be threatened. In early January 1943, a group of Unionist MPs formally demanded the appointment of a new and younger ministerial team. Like his predecessor, Andrews obstinately resisted, hoping that a resolute, uncompromising stand might force his critics to retreat. He acted partly from loyalty to old colleagues, who had enjoyed the confidence of Craig and, in some cases, even Carson. But he was also motivated by political weakness; he publicly claimed that the members of his cabinet were the best available whilst privately he recognised and was concerned about their inadequacies. Some of them made it clear that they would only leave office 'in a box'.

In the background, paralysing labour disputes in Belfast and two IRA prison break-outs further eroded Andrews's credibility. Eventually, on 28 April 1943, he tendered his resignation at a meeting of the Unionist parliamentary party. It was evident that otherwise six, mainly junior, ministers would have resigned and the party might well have been irretrievably split.

His successor was Sir Basil Brooke (premier, 1 May 1942-24 March 1963), an Anglo-Irish landlord from County Fermanagh. It is unlikely that anyone else would have had sufficient Commons support to form a government. He was regarded by the nationalist minority as a bigot; during 1933-4 he had made a series of intemperate speeches in which he 'appealed to loyalists ... wherever possible, to employ Protestant lads and lassies'. Nonetheless, in 1943, he had much to offer the Unionist party. By Stormont standards, he was young (fifty-four years old) and had a considerable breadth of experience.

Brooke appointed new, little-known but generally competent ministers, including Harry Midgley of the Labour Party, the first non-unionist to reach cabinet rank. From the outset, the premier's obsession (an undoubted source of weakness) was to restore and maintain party unity. On taking office, he therefore tried to improve the party's morale and cohesion in a variety of ways. These included modernising its organisation (the British Conservative party was his model), improving governmental 'publicity', inviting leading British politicians over to Belfast, attempting to win over Andrews and his sacked cabinet colleagues, restoring the functions of Belfast Corporation and generally trying to avoid divisive legislation, at least in wartime.

Brooke was also responsive to the changing mood of the electorate. Apart from the maintenance of the Constitution, his government's two agreed priorities were to bring greater drive to the war effort and to devise plans for the post-war years. He publicly committed himself to a policy of full employment and to follow Westminster in implementing the terms of the

Beveridge Report, which included provision for a comprehensive National Insurance system to eradicate poverty and a health service. He appointed a minister with responsibility for preparing a programme to be implemented when hostilities ended. The first-ever enquiries were held to quantify how far Northern Ireland lagged behind Great Britain in health, education and housing, and legislation was introduced which was intended to attract new industry when peace returned.

After mid-1944, apprehension amongst ministers soared as munitions contracts became fewer and the major industrial firms began to lay off sections of their workforce. Their concern was that post-war unemployment would rapidly reach 1930s levels; it doubled between September and December 1944. They were convinced that if it remained higher than in Great Britain the government would not survive.

This background helps account for Brooke's continued commitment to conscription. In 1945, he became aware that Westminster planned to retain compulsory military service (i.e. National Service) after hostilities had ended and he urged that it be extended to Northern Ireland as well. This appealed to him partly on political grounds, as its introduction would underline the region's constitutional status within the Union. But he was also aware that it would in itself lower unemployment levels by mopping up surplus labour. Moreover, he hoped that accepting the obligations of common citizenship would enable Britain to treat the Six Counties more generously, by contributing to the mounting cost of its social services and facilitating its efforts to achieve full employment. Such was his enthusiasm for this policy that he favoured making a discreet approach to the Catholic hierarchy to establish whether more generous public funding of church schools would soften its traditionally hostile response.

British ministers rejected Brooke's request outright; in their view, he had made no case at all. They considered that it would be quite indefensible for Westminster to impose conscription for economic reasons and that for Stormont to introduce it at a time when there was no risk to the conscripts would invite ridicule and opprobrium. Moreover, its application was not thought to be in the best interest of Northern Ireland itself. It was regarded as likely to 'provoke rebellion ... by a large minority who can always look for support from across the border'.

Despite this, by 1945, relations between Westminster and Stormont governments had become closer than at any time in their history. This was not due primarily to any outstanding commitment shown or sacrifice made in wartime by the parliament or people of Northern Ireland. Its voluntary recruitment levels were a constant source of disappointment, even embarrassment, to Stormont ministers. When Britain had faced defeat in 1940 and Craig was invited to enter into discussions with de Valera, he had without compunction placed the interests of Northern Ireland and the preservation of the Union above loyalty to King and Empire. The major local munitions firms performed poorly, especially during 1939-42. At Short & Harland aircraft factory, output was then three times slower than at comparable producers elsewhere in the United Kingdom. It was estimated that the roughly 20,000 strong workforce at Harland & Wolff shipyard was manufacturing the equivalent of just 12,000 workers in Great Britain during the early stages of the war.

Northern Ireland's War Effort

Nonetheless by 1945 Northern Ireland had made a significant cumulative contribution to the overall war effort. It produced, for example, 270 ships, 1,500 aircraft, 75 millions shells and met roughly one-third of War Office demand for rope and 90 percent of British armed forces' shirt requirements. Its farmers provided cattle and sheep to the value of £3 million annually and 20 percent of the total supplies of home-produced eggs (360 million in 1944 alone).

In all, 38,000 men and women from the area volunteered for service and an impressive list of British army generals were of Ulster (nine counties) extraction, including Alexander, Auchinleck, Brooke, Dill and Montgomery. In the course of the conflict almost 6,000 people from the Six Counties lost their lives, either killed in action or due to Luftwaffe attack. The experience of 1914-18, when huge casualty levels were sustained at the Somme, was not repeated. During 1939-45 the death toll rose gradually. After virtually every major military engagement, names appeared in the obituary columns of local newspapers.

However, Northern Ireland's geographical position lay at the root of its true significance in the Second World War. Herbert Morrison, a member of the British cabinet, commented that her 'strategic position alone ensures that her contribution is a crucial one'. As a result of German conquest of Western Europe and southern Ireland's neutrality (Britain did not, therefore, have access to their harbours and airfields), the Six Counties was the most westerly area in Allied hands. Churchill stated that when the Axis powers sought to 'strangle our life by cutting off the entry to our ports', Northern Ireland provided a 'safe' conduit for the food and war material flooding in from the United States and Canada. He wrote: 'Only one great channel of entry remained open ... Loyal Ulster gave us full use of the North [sic] Irish ports and waters. But for its loyalty ... we should have been confronted with slavery and death.' Its role, especially in the Battle of the Atlantic, was vital. It became a base for convoys, escorts, maritime reconnaissance, Coastal Command and anti-submarine aircraft. Its availability, according to Morrison, helped narrow the 'unprotected gap in mid-Atlantic, the stretch of water which could not be covered by shore-based aircraft from either side'.

In addition, the area served as a training ground and launching pad for some of the great military offensives in the European theatre of war. Over 300,000 US and other Allied service personnel (including 25,000 Belgian troops) saw wartime duty in Northern Ireland. On 26 January 1942, six weeks after Pearl Harbour, American divisions disembarked at Dufferin Quay in Belfast. It was a milestone in the course of the conflict; they were the first GIs officially to set foot in Europe in the Second World War. During May 1942, their strength reached 37,000, just before their participation in 'Operation Torch' against Axis forces in North Africa and Italy.

During the autumn of 1943, a second wave arrived in preparation for the opening up of a second front in Western Europe. Immediately prior to the Normandy landings (June 1944) their numbers reached over 120,000; numerous airfields (18 were in operation at the end of the war), military camps and barracks were constructed to accommodate them. Afterwards General Eisenhower stated: 'Without Northern Ireland, I do not see how American forces could have been concentrated to begin the invasion.'

Meanwhile Westminster's changed view of Northern Ireland's strategic importance and appreciation of its wartime role influenced its policy decisively both during and after the war. Churchill was not alone in concluding that 'a strong, loyal Ulster will always be vital to the security and well-being of our whole empire'. In 1949, this perspective received legislative expression in the guarantee then given by Britain that the region would remain within the Union for as long as a majority in the parliament at Stormont wished. Earlier, during negotiations in 1943-1944, the Treasury had agreed to raise substantially its level of financial support to the Six Counties, so enabling it to implement fully the Beveridge Report and also to catch up with social welfare provision elsewhere in the United Kingdom in such vital areas as education, health and housing. This concession formed the basis of the region's total transformation after 1945.

Whilst the governments in London and Belfast drew closer between 1939 and 1945, there is little to suggest that any comparable improvement took place then in sectarian relations within Northern Ireland. It is, of course, true that the border issue receded during the conflict. Initially, Protestants and Catholics shared some aspects of wartime experience. They served as ARP wardens, fire-watchers and rescue workers and fled in terror after the Belfast blitz or huddled together during the hours of darkness in suburban hedgerows and ditches. One of the most enduring folk memories from the war years is of women and children from both the Shankill and the Falls gathering in the vaults of Clonard monastery during early May whilst the Luftwaffe pulverised the streets outside. The Redemptorist priests had opened their property to the local community, whatever their religion, for want of alternative shelter in the area.

But, after the air-raids, the unclaimed dead were buried in separate graveyards, according to their presumed faith – a potent image in itself of deep sectarian division. Also, wartime attitudes divided sharply along traditional lines. Northern nationalists were notably less enthusiastic about the war. Their perspective was influenced by the fact of Irish neutrality but essentially most felt no inclination to fight for a government whose existence they opposed. They were therefore hostile to conscription and under-represented in the civil defence services. Moreover, they were generally antagonistic towards United States troops, because their units strengthened the forces of law and order and could be used to enforce partition or even invade the South. Some IRA activity continued, especially during 1940-42. By June 1940, 155 suspects had been interned and, on 2 September 1942, the first republican execution in Northern Ireland history occurred. The accused was sentenced to death by hanging, having been found guilty of shooting dead a police officer.

Unionist Party suspicion of nationalists continued unabated throughout the conflict. Its members tended to regard them as a sort of fifth column – pro-German and anti-British by instinct and tradition – whose grievances were not as great as they protested. Party resolutions focused on the alleged 'danger' of their getting jobs in the post office, civil service or industry, exploiting the absence of loyalists who had joined Crown forces or migrated to work in English munitions factories. The more active wartime role played by Protestants was used by some to justify illiberal policies, such as the allocation of houses to them rather than to Catholics who might well be in greater need. The Stormont government's suspicion of and insensitivity towards the minority is illustrated by its use of Unionist Party officials when conducting military recruitment drives and of the Special Constabulary as the nucleus for the local home guard.

Policy on the Minority

But Brooke's policies were by no means exclusively determined by narrow prejudice. His commitment to full employment post-1945 and to the implementation of the Beveridge Report was partly because he was convinced that 'the only chance for the political future of Ulster ... is if she becomes so prosperous that the traditional political barriers are broken down'. On occasion he and his colleagues sought to thwart rather than indulge sectarian pressures. For example, a Housing Trust was created in early 1945 to counteract the rampant discrimination practised by local authorities whatever their political complexion. It was legally obliged to provide and allocate working-class houses, adhering strictly to an objective points system based on need, and is regarded as having been a successful and worthwhile initiative.

When the cabinet debated educational reform, Brooke advocated generosity towards Catholic-controlled schools on the grounds that the children 'must be the first consideration'. Patrick Shea, who worked in the Ministry of Education, considered that the cabinet had a well-deserved reputation for generosity towards Catholic schools after the war, when in his view they made exceptional progress. In 1945, it was also decided that family allowances should be provided on precisely the same terms as in Great Britain, even though it was evident that the minority would benefit disproportionately from this due to its higher birth rate.

The proportion of Catholics living in Northern Ireland rose, though only slowly, between 1926 and 1961 (from 33.4 percent to 34.9 percent), mainly because they accounted for approximately 55 percent of all emigration during these years. Brooke could see no solution to the growing 'disloyal' population other than by improving Northern Ireland's prosperity. However, his government responded to the perceived threat indirectly by closely monitoring southern Irish labour coming north to work. It did so by issuing residence permits under powers derived from the Home Office in London. They considered allowing politically loyal southerners to stay but not surprisingly found it impossible to formulate a practicable scheme. When it seemed that Westminster might not sanction this system of regulation to continue after the war, some ministers favoured the drastic action of having the 1920 Government of Ireland Act amended so as to provide Stormont with the necessary powers. Brooke described the matter as a 'burning question'; and one which he believed could, if not resolved satisfactorily, jeopardise the Union.

CHAPTER 6

The Post-War Swing to the Left

During the euphoria of VE Day (8 May 1945), Brooke consulted his colleagues at Stormont; after brief discussion, they decided to go to the polls at once before the problems of the post-war world could become evident to the local electorate. Their apprehension about the outcome was fully justified. When the election was held on 14 June the unionist share of the vote dropped to 50.4 percent, its second lowest level since 1921. In contrast, Labour representatives amassed a stunning 31.9 percent of the total (8.6 percent in 1933 had been their previous best) and five candidates were returned.

From a unionist perspective, worse was to come; the wartime swing to the left was even more striking three weeks later on 5 July, when the British Labour party won its first-ever outright majority at Westminster. Its unexpected victory sent a shudder of alarm through members of the Stormont cabinet. Brooke recorded privately their fears that they would now be 'compelled to adopt very strong socialist measures'; some considered that a major crisis in inter-governmental relations would be unavoidable. An additional worry was that the socialist administration would exert powerful pressure on Northern Ireland to accept Dublin rule; in Brooke's word, '[we] may be forced into the Free State'. His feelings of unease were reinforced by the observable rise in expectations within the northern minority following Attlee's triumph; it prompted Nationalist MPs to take their seats again in the Belfast parliament.

In retrospect, it is clear that both Northern Ireland communities benefited greatly from the policies of the new British government even though, like its predecessors, it took little active interest in Irish affairs and was equally anxious to avoid entanglements there. Some of its members initially made disparaging comments publicly about the Unionist Party. Home Secretary Chuter Ede described it as 'remnants of the old ascendancy, very frightened of the Roman Catholics and the world trend to the left'.

Nonetheless, the socialist ministers overall were sympathetic in their attitude towards the Stormont leadership. Occasionally they expressed concern that electoral procedures in the Six Counties fell below 'British standards of democracy', but they acknowledged and respected the fact that a large and genuine majority there strongly favoured union with Britain. They were also highly appreciative of the North's wartime role, which they compared favourably with the South's neutrality, and regarded it as vital to Allied victory. (Philip Noel-Baker at the Dominions Office stated categorically that without Northern Ireland's help 'Hitler would undoubtedly have won ... and [we] would have been defeated'. Moreover, they were convinced that their keen sense of gratitude was widely shared within the British electorate. Whilst the experience of war had made them acutely conscious of the North's strategic importance to Britain, ultimately they favoured Irish unification – within the Empire. They regarded it as 'inevitable'; their concern was that it be brought about gradually and without coercion.

Fears of a 'Socialist System'

At first some inter-governmental friction arose, mainly because Labour ministers began to intervene more in Northern Irish affairs than the unionist leadership had come to expect from Westminster. Soon, however, Brooke came to regard them as 'punctilious in refusing to be drawn into any discussion on matters falling within [his government's] jurisdiction' under the 1920 Act. This was true even in the most sensitive of areas – electoral law, local government boundaries, the application of emergency powers – and despite the appeals of Irish nationalists and the protests of Labour back-benchers.

British policy with regard to the economy remained by far the most enduring cause of Unionist concern – in particular, the rash of nationalisation schemes, the general trends towards centralisation and the continuation of rationing and of wartime controls and regulations (regarding capital investment, raw material allocation, etc). Stormont ministers harboured dark suspicions that the Westminster government was 'using the (post-war) crisis' to create a 'socialist system'. This they were opposed to on grounds of principle; they also considered that they had no mandate for such a policy, that it would irreparably damage the northern economy and threatened to undermine the independence of the regional parliament.

In response, some argued passionately for a change in the North's constitutional position so as to increase its independence from Britain; the 'Dominion status' granted to southern Ireland in the Treaty (6 December 1921) was regarded as a possible alternative. Given the region's growing dependence on financial support from the Treasury, however, this has never proved to be a feasible option; in 1946, northern farmers alone were receiving Exchequer grants worth £13 million per annum. In Brooke's opinion, therefore, there was 'no practical alternative' but to co-operate with Britain as closely as possible, leaving the 1920 settlement un-changed.

The Welfare State

The tensions within the Unionist party resulting from this policy were eased by the fact that the Labour government treated Northern Ireland more generously than any previous Westminster administration. Within months of taking office, it sanctioned a trebling of pre-war levels of expenditure on the Special Constabulary. At the time, the Inspector General described the Six Counties as 'one of the few peaceful spots in the world'.

More crucially, the socialist leadership honoured Britain's wartime commitments by signing two agreements, in 1946 and 1949, which recognised Northern Ireland's right and funded its efforts to maintain its social services at the same levels as elsewhere in the United Kingdom. Brooke and his colleagues initiated the necessary legislation with genuine enthusiasm, prompting Herbert Morrison (Lord President) to describe them as behaving like 'moderate socialists'. Their positive response was related to the Treasury's generous support and their awareness that the reform measures were sorely needed to eradicate poverty and raise basic standards of health. Also, since 1922, Stormont's broad objective had consistently been to match Westminster 'step by step' in welfare provision. Unionist leaders had constantly feared that if they did otherwise Protestant workers would defect from the party to Labour. A further political calculation was that if a gap in social services could be created between North and South it would provide a potent additional argument for preserving the Union.

Collectively, the reforms introduced in the late 1940s transformed Northern Ireland and resulted in a massive increase in public expenditure. In 1952, the Stormont government was spending over £30 million on social services (four times the pre-war figure). In that year, over 550,000 workers were covered by its National Insurance scheme and were receiving benefits and pensions costing over £10 million per year; roughly 60,000 persons were claiming national assistance, amounting to £3.5 million in total, and family allowances were being claimed for 216,000 children at an annual expenditure of £2.7 million. William Grant, the minister responsible, justifiably described these measures as 'the great experiment'. Combined with the setting up of a National Health Service (according to Brooke, it was 'ahead of anything in England') and a Tuberculosis Authority, they contributed to a dramatic fall in the local death rate. It had been the highest in the United Kingdom in 1939; by 1954 it was below the average for England and Wales and, by 1962, was lower than in any other region in Great Britain. Before then, the urban scourge of TB had been so far eradicated that the Authority was dissolved in 1959.

Meanwhile, the first significant steps since partition had been taken in response to Northern Ireland's acute housing shortage. The area had a total post-war stock of 323,000 houses; on some government estimates as many as 200,000 further dwellings were urgently required. Slow initial progress prompted one talented, but frustrated, young minister, Maynard Sinclair, to offer his resignation, as he felt his best efforts were 'not effective'. However, legislation passed in 1945 eventually led to a doubling of the pre-war rate of construction; by 1955, 58,000 houses had been completed.

Education, like health and housing, had also hitherto suffered serious neglect, partly because the service was, in Brooke's words, political 'dynamite'. The 1947 Education Act was a legislative milestone; it made secondary education free and compulsory for all. Though the measure introduced, as in Britain, dubious selection procedures based on the 'eleven plus' qualifying examination (its purpose, then as now, was to distinguish between academic and non-academic children at the age of eleven), it was a major step towards equality of opportunity for all and had in due course significant political repercussions locally. Eighty percent of those attending grammar schools (i.e. the academic stream) were provided with scholarships and university grants were available to all with sufficient proven ability. By 1952, the number of secondary school children (42,500) was almost four times pre-war levels and again increased sharply when the school-leaving age was raised to 15 in 1957.

Minority and Social Reform

A consequence of these social reforms was that they dramatically heightened the region's financial dependence on Westminster and so potentially strengthened its hold over Stormont; this was little considered at the time given the warmth of inter-governmental relations. More obviously, implementation of the measures and the resulting expansion of state control raised very sensitive political issues in Northern Ireland, which had no real equivalent in Britain. Some of the decisions taken by local ministers reinforced the perception amongst Catholics that the authorities were hostile to their interests.

For example, when setting up the health service, the government encouraged private hospitals to transfer control to the Northern Ireland Hospitals Board. The Mater Infirmorum, a Catholic church-owned 200-bed teaching hospital in Belfast, founded in 1883, refused to do so whatever inducements or guarantees were offered. Its representatives stated categorically that Canon Law 'forbade the handing over of a hospital to any authority'. Brooke and his colleagues expressed surprise, as this difficulty had not apparently arisen in Britain, but were equally obdurate; they had agreed in cabinet at the outset that there could be 'no half measures'. Given their attitude, compromise proved impossible. As a result the Mater lost its entitlement even to those grants it had received before the formation of the NHS; it retained its voluntary status and survived exclusively on private donations until the stalemate was finally resolved in 1972.

Similarly, Catholic church-owned schools stated that 'under no circumstances' would they transfer control to the Local Education Authorities (under the 1947 Act). A delegation of bishops and clergy stated that 'they would return to hedge schools' rather than admit the LEAs to a share in the management of their institutions. The problem was complicated further for northern ministers by the advice which they received from their Attorney General. He indicated that the main terms of their education legislation were in effect illegal, as they were 'tantamount to the endowment of Protestantism'. This had also been the case with the measures passed in the inter-war years.

On making enquiries, they were advised by the Home Office in London that it would intervene only if it received complaints from the northern minority. It was in order to forestall this possibility that Brooke and his colleagues raised the scale of grants to Catholic schools from the 50 percent offered initially to 65 percent (i.e. 65 percent of all capital expenditure on buildings, maintenance finance, heating, lighting, etc. Teachers' salaries were paid in full throughout). This level of support was higher than had ever been offered before and more than would have been available to such schools in England and Wales. Backbench Unionist outrage at this generosity eventually forced Hall-Thompson, the minister responsible, to resign.

Brooke himself estimated that Catholic pupils at the time represented 37 percent of the total school population and that they would receive 29 percent of public expenditure on education. He thought this reasonable, as Catholic Church control over its schools remained intact and, had it been willing to dilute this control, government funding would have increased accordingly. The hierarchy protested vehemently, however, that it should receive full 100 percent grants. It justified this claim on the grounds that the minority paid its full share of taxes and rates and was therefore 'entitled to parity with Protestants, whether under the LEA or not'. It also argued that the favourable comparisons being drawn by ministers with practice in England were irrelevant, given that the Catholic community comprised over one-third of the population in the Six Counties. Overall, both the health and education reforms suggested to Catholics that they were being required to pay extra for the maintenance of their religious beliefs and practices. This inevitably lessened the positive impact of the legislation on local community relations.

No 'One Man, One Vote'

Few aspects of political life in the Six Counties escaped accusations of sectarian bias. The local government franchise became an issue of extreme controversy after Stormont's decision, in 1946, not to follow Westminster precedent by introducing 'one man, one vote'. Under Northern Ireland legislation, lodgers, children away from home, servants and those living in rented property in the Six Counties were not enfranchised. The Home Office considered that these terms were 'designed drastically to effect the composition' of councils in border areas by reducing the nationalist electorate; present-day historians have tended to agree. Ministers summoned to London to justify their measure strongly denied this accusation. From their arguments, it seems likely that, as in the 1920s, the Unionist leadership was as much concerned by the electoral threat posed by Labour groups, particularly in view of their remarkable performance in the 1945 contest. When Brooke sought to convince sceptical backbenchers that it would be a mistake to emulate Britain, he stressed that to do so 'would mean the loss to the ... party of many towns and cities'. In any case, he considered it 'perfectly fair' that the vote should be restricted broadly to those who paid rates.

Impact of Welfare Reforms

Despite claims of unfairness regarding their implementation, the major post-war social reforms helped to provide a framework for Northern Ireland's stability, at least in the short-term, and to generate encouraging signs of social integration, reconciliation and increased tolerance in the 1950s and 1960s. This was as Brooke had hoped and intended. Arguably, bolder, more generous policies by northern ministers might have helped really to bridge the sectarian divide and lay the foundations for permanent peace. Alternatively, it may be that the difficulties in fully reconciling the nationalist community and inducing its acceptance of the legitimacy of the State were ultimately insuperable. Certainly, their resolution would have required not just improved welfare provision but a root-and-branch reform of Northern Ireland's institutions to eradicate any trace of discrimination.

The 'Republic of Ireland'

Apart from providing liberal financial assistance to the North, Labour ministers made another important but more controversial contribution to its post-war stability. In 1949 they passed legislation which appeared appreciably to strengthen its constitutional position within the Union. Ironically, the measure was a direct consequence of the decision taken by J A Costello's Dublin government to sever the South's remaining ties with Britain and its Empire. With effect from Easter (8 April) 1949, Éire became the fully independent 'Republic of Ireland'.

The change had important political repercussions. It caused considerable excitement amongst nationalists throughout the island, which found expression in a virulent anti-partition campaign into the early 1950s; unity seemed the next logical step – the only 'unfinished business' left to the nation's leaders. Lord Rugby, British Ambassador in Dublin, feared that this rising tide of emotion would lead to the gun being brought back into Irish politics.

Brooke capitalised on the inflamed political tensions by holding an election on 10 February 1949, on the single issue: 'Whether we are King's men or not' (i.e. do voters wish to maintain the Union with Britain or not). He hoped to arrest and reverse the post-war swing to the left. He could legitimately claim that the outcome was a 'magnificent victory'. The unionist vote rose 12 percent from 1945 (and its Commons majority from 14 to 22). The Prime Minister also achieved his main objective – the Labour Party challenge withered. Its candidates were the foremost casualties of the contest, its support fell to roughly one-third of its 1945 peak. Two months later, therefore, after twenty-five years of equivocation on the partition issue, Labour vowed henceforth to 'maintain unbroken the connection' with Great Britain.

Ulster Unionism derived other benefits from Costello's decision, which he neither foresaw nor intended. It resulted in legislation at Westminster (the Ireland Act) to acknowledge formally and ratify legally the change in Éire's status. Stormont ministers seized every opportunity to influence the bill's content, in order to 'protect and strengthen the political position' of the Belfast parliament in its dealings both with London and Dublin. They were anxious to exploit, in Rugby's phrase, a 'favourable moment in history'; the recent wartime role of the Six Counties guaranteed a broadly sympathetic hearing at Westminster for their proposals.

Brooke's main argument was that his supporters needed political reassurance; he claimed that Éire's secession from the Empire and the associated strident pro-unity campaign had caused uncertainty in Unionist minds. His most important request was that in these circumstances some unsolicited remarks made by Attlee in the Commons (in October and November 1948) should be written into the legislation being prepared. The Labour leader had said that there should be 'no change in the constitutional status of Northern Ireland without Northern Ireland's agreement'.

The Guarantee to Northern Ireland

In subsequent negotiations, the socialist cabinet accepted the Unionist position; it was agreed that a 'declaratory clause' should be written into the bill stating that the North would remain within the Union for as long as a majority at Stormont wished. Its inclusion is usually regarded as one of Brooke's foremost achievements; but in fact Attlee needed no persuasion. He was anxious to allay Unionist fears, which he regarded as legitimate and genuine. Also, he believed that the inclusion of the proposed clause would be popular with the British electorate. Above all, he was convinced that it was in Britain's best interests. His leading officials had advised him that, in view of Éire's secession from the Empire and in the light of the recent experience of war, it was 'a matter of first-class strategic importance for this country that the North should continue to form part of His Majesty's dominions. So far as can be foreseen, it will never be to Great Britain's advantage that Northern Ireland should form part of a territory outside His Majesty's jurisdiction. Indeed it is unlikely that Great Britain would ever be able to agree to this, even if the people of Northern Ireland desired it.'

Attlee accepted just one other request of substance from the Stormont leadership – the introduction of a three-month residence qualification into Northern Ireland for those seeking to register for the vote in

Westminster elections there. He agreed to this because he had been convinced that there was otherwise a risk of substantial numbers of southern Irishmen crossing into the North, with the aim of overturning the Unionist majority. However improbable, he considered this to be a possible stratagem in the anti-partition campaign. He did, meanwhile, dismiss one of Brooke's other suggestions – that Westminster refuse to adopt the change of title which Costello was introducing. Stormont ministers argued that the use of the new nomenclature (i.e. 'Republic of Ireland') would imply recognition and acceptance of the South's claim to jurisdiction over the Six Counties. But Attlee considered that to reject it would cause unnecessary resentment in Éire and amongst Irishmen living in the Commonwealth; in any case, he considered it to be an impracticable, undignified and hair-splitting response.

Reaction to the Ireland Act

Reaction to the Ireland Act was more or less predictable. Southern leaders protested vehemently against the declaratory clause, tending to ignore other terms which treated the Republic generously. They interpreted it as indicative of an alarming shift in Britain's policy to one of uncompromising support for partition. In contrast, Stormont ministers were delighted with it; Brooke stated privately: 'It places the fate of Ulster in our own hands. We have got what we wanted.'

Within the Labour cabinet, however, a minority regarded the assurances given to the North with deep misgivings. These members considered it unwise to place the future of the Union in the hands of the Belfast parliament; given its reputation for the gerrymandering of local government boundaries, they doubted (with little justification) that it fairly represented the opinions of the Northern Ireland electorate. Lord Longford alone opposed strongly and on principle the inclusion of the guarantee Brooke had requested; for him unity was the only solution to the Irish question. Philip Noel-Baker (Dominions Office) also thought it 'short-sighted ... to continue partition and thereby alienate the natural sympathy of the Irish people'. He considered that the 'present situation [would] not last' and the British government itself realised that 'sooner or later there will be a united Ireland'.

CHAPTER 7

Northern Ireland's 'Best Years'

The 1950s and early 1960s were Northern Ireland's most harmonious and most promising years, broadly characterised by economic growth, steady social improvement and a unique degree of peace and stability. In hindsight, it acquired for many the aura of a golden age; the *Annual Register* described political life at the time as 'unexciting'. A key underlying cause was the spectacular growth in public expenditure. Stormont was spending over 20 percent of the region's GNP in 1950 and this proportion was rising. The net capital transfer from Britain to the Six Counties had reached £46 million by 1962 and over £70 million by 1968. Liberal financial inducements to employers, provided by government, helped keep unemployment at a comparatively low 7-8 percent. Almost 60,000 houses were constructed in the 1950s and the number of secondary school pupils doubled. By 1965, £22 million had been spent on hospital provision since the war and a further £44 million was earmarked for future development.

In contrast, the immediate post-war years were a period of crisis for the twenty-six counties. As the Unionist leaders had hoped, a gap in economic and social development opened between the Republic and Northern Ireland. In the north, industry grew at 2.1 percent yearly in the 1950s, compared with 1.3 percent in the south. At the same time agricultural prices in the latter were on average 10 percent lower than over the border. Its rural areas were described as 'stricken and dying'; between 1951 and 1961, the number of adult males employed on its farms fell by one-fifth.

Whilst the total population of the North rose by 50,000 during the decade, in Éire it fell by 5 percent (23 percent for the 20-34 age group) and 500,000 of its citizens emigrated between 1945 and 1960. Welfare payments were on average 50 percent higher in the Six Counties by the early 1960s. Fear of southerners crossing over to take advantage of its higher benefits were reflected in the inclusion by Stormont of a residence qualification for those claiming family allowances or support under the national insurance and national assistance schemes. Though the population of Northern Ireland was less than half that of the Republic, it had then 10,000 more pupils at secondary school and spent three times more on higher education. For the Dublin government to have raised its social services to Northern standards would have required more than a doubling of its current expenditure. For it to have taken over Britain's financial commitments in the North, it would have had to increase its taxation levels by as much as 60 percent.

Unionist Views of the New Republic

These circumstances were bound to have political implications. Along with the declaratory clause in the Ireland Act, they made for an increased sense of security and of confidence amongst Unionists. In speeches at the time, party leaders frequently boasted of the 'assets' which they claimed 'Ulster' derived from the Union, particularly economic strength and parity of social services. They depicted the North as modernising, expanding and building on its wartime role by playing a full part in the Western Defence Union and offering a potential base for NATO troops in the Cold War. They contrasted this with the allegedly backward, stagnant, internationally-marginalised South; its war-time isolation was being preserved by high tariffs and a policy of non-alignment towards Europe.

Brooke issued appeals to the minority to recognise that 'unity would be disastrous' and to Éire to show 'realism'. In the Unionist mantra, Catholicism was portrayed as destructive of international greatness and corrosive of individual rights and personal freedom; this, it was suggested, was indicated by the levels of censorship in the Republic and by its minimal economic growth. Stormont ministers also began to express stronger pro-British sentiments than in the past. Just as they had done before the war, they claimed to share with Britain the same democratic values and liberal principles. Their feelings of patriotism, however, had since been sharpened by the shared experience of war and post-war progress towards parity in welfare provision. Unionists derived satisfaction from Westminster's apparent esteem for the region as evidenced by the 'declaratory clause' of the Ireland Act, the Treasury's consistently liberal financial support and the generally close level of inter-governmental co-operation.

Increased confidence and greater security inevitably also influenced unionist attitudes towards the minority. A small but growing number of party members, drawn especially from the Protestant middle class, became more tolerant in approach, more vocal and more influential; there had always been a more liberal tradition within the movement. In the 1950s this was expressed in an increased willingness to accept the need for gradual reform in Northern Ireland and, in particular, to change the nature of the party itself by enrolling Catholics as members and even adopting them as parliamentary candidates. These views were supported in speeches (November 1959) by Sir Clarence Graham,

Chairman of the party's standing committee and a member of its executive, and by Brian Maginess, then Attorney General, when addressing a Young Unionist conference. Maginess stated that 'to broaden our outlook means no weakening of our faith. Toleration is not a sign of weakness but proof of strength.'

Minority Attitudes Change

Meanwhile, Brooke's hopes that social reform and economic growth might lessen nationalist hostility towards partition also seemed to be at least partially fulfilled. Already in 1951, Maginess declared: 'We are weakening the anti-partition movement ... [Catholics] ... are gradually coming to have faith in us, our permanent constitutional position, our fair administration.'

The Catholic middle class expanded after the war due to the steady improvement in education services and in job prospects. Government success in attracting new industry to Northern Ireland opened up employment opportunities in management and administration. At the same time the Catholic working class benefited, often disproportionately, from developments in welfare provision (such as family allowances) and likewise from the arrival of subsidiaries of British- and foreign-owned firms, which were less likely to practise religious discrimination in appointments than local employers.

There were now indications within both Catholic social groups of a greater willingness to accept partition, at least in the short term, whilst still not abandoning their long-term aspiration to unity. A significant section of the minority became more reconciled to Northern institutions than before; it entered more fully and constructively into local politics seeking reform to eliminate discrimination, establish more fully democratic institutions and perhaps even initiate some form of power sharing. This, in essence, was the approach of National Unity, a forerunner of the SDLP, formed in 1959 by Catholic middle-class graduates in Belfast. Such elements were also more critical of the South; one of their spokesmen in 1958, dismissed the Republic's claim to be the *de jure* government of the North and stated that Catholics had a duty 'to co-operate with the *de facto* authority there that controls life and welfare'.

A revival in the fortunes of various left-wing candidates for the Belfast parliament was a further symptom of Catholic amelioration. Representatives of the Northern Ireland Labour Party and other Labour groupings won six seats in the 1958 contest, seven in 1962, and received respectively 28.7 percent and 32.8 percent of the total poll. Their improved performance was due in part to an upturn in unemployment and the absence of any distracting border scare or crisis to polarise voters. But, above all, it was caused by the increased backing which they received from the Catholic working-class; it provided roughly two-thirds of Labour's electoral support. As the Northern Ireland Labour Party had declared itself to be unambiguously in favour of partition in 1949, this suggested that 'the union was no longer anathema to Catholic voters'.

IRA Campaign Fails

The failure of the IRA campaign (12 December 1956-26 February 1962) also indicated that minority attitudes were changing. The force had been both devastated and demoralised by wartime internment but had recovered sufficiently by the early 1950s for its younger members to favour ending the prolonged post-war period of inaction. In keeping with republican tradition, this intention was signalled by a series of daring arms raids on military barracks (at Derry, Armagh and Omagh and in England), beginning in 1951. Amongst the security measures taken in response, Sir Basil Brooke was given a heavier police guard and instructed to switch cars and vary his travel times and routes.

The campaign proper began against the backcloth of the Suez crisis and the Hungarian uprising. The volunteers adopted strictly guerrilla tactics, attacked property within the Six Counties exclusively and sought scrupulously to avoid civilian bloodshed. Over the six-year period, they were involved in roughly 600 violent incidents, mainly attacks on RUC stations, government property, bridges and essential services. Owing to lack of men and equipment, many were on so minor a scale as to amount to 'mere vandalism' (such as blowing up telephone kiosks, etc). Nonetheless, by 1962, eighteen people had died, twelve of them IRA members.

The campaign failed, partly because of the effective security measures taken by both Irish governments. Northern ministers introduced internment in 1956 (arresting in total 335 suspects), and in 1957 de Valera did likewise, eventually imprisoning virtually the entire republican leadership. But the IRA decision to cease activities was also taken because of its inability to attract sufficient popular support. The explanatory statement which it issued in 1962 referred to the indifferent 'attitude of the general public'; this factor had consistently sapped morale and contributed to self-defeating internal divisions. It had also given the unionist cabinet sufficient confidence to release the internees long before the hostilities had formally ended. All had been freed by late 1960.

As Brooke had hoped, the firm measures taken by

Stormont helped forestall random loyalist reprisals against Catholic areas or 'counter-attacks' across the border; either would undoubtedly have bolstered minority support for republican violence. In addition, the Catholic hierarchy condemned membership of the IRA as a 'mortal sin', so further diminishing its appeal. Overall, the number of votes cast for Sinn Féin, the force's political wing, halved between the 1955 and 1959 elections, falling from 152,000 votes to 74,000. The party's political programme, which condemned the welfare state as an assault on the freedom of the individual, can have done little to enhance its popular appeal. Long before the 1956-1962 campaign had ended, its main purpose had become to keep the spirit of Easter 1916 and of militant republicanism alive; in this limited objective it was certainly successful.

Inter-Communal Integration

Evidence of more tolerant unionist attitudes and of the minority becoming more reconciled to partition coincided with an increasing level of intermingling and of integration between the two communities; this was especially the case within the middle class. Opportunities for social contact between the two traditions expanded with the growth in leisure activities, golf and tennis clubs, drama and music societies, young farmers' unions, etc. Also within higher education the proportion of Catholic undergraduates at Queen's University had risen from 5 percent pre-1914 to 22 percent by the late 1950s. Religious segregation in housing also became less acute, particularly in the wealthier suburban areas. Within the working class, both the trade union movement and the mainstream Labour political organisations generally opposed sectarianism and provided a limited outlet for inter-sectional social contact.

However, despite some encouraging signs of progress during the immediate post-war decades, Northern Ireland was still nowhere near to having become a stable democracy. At no time was the minority reconciled to the State. In 1951, therefore, concern about security prompted the Governor, Lord Glanville, to voice strong objections to proceeding with a proposed royal visit. His views were ignored. But Stormont ministers later noted with dismay the 'ironic cheers' and sullen atmosphere when Princess Elizabeth approached nationalist areas. These the Princess herself chose regally to ignore; instead she 'mentioned' to Brooke 'the friendship she noticed here and, in fact, in crossing the sea she noticed no difference'. Later in the decade during the IRA campaign, electoral support for anti-partition parties dropped sharply but it had already revived measurably even before a ceasefire had been declared.

Nationalist candidates for Westminster attracted 14.5 percent, 18 percent and 21 percent of the poll respectively in the 1959, 1964 and 1966 contests. In Stormont elections, constituencies with a Catholic majority show a similar pattern in 1962 and 1965, whilst the proportion of votes and seats won by nationalists on Belfast City Council rose steadily through the 1960s. The uncompromising spirit of Easter 1916 clearly retained a resonance within minority areas. In the 1953 Stormont election, the Sinn Féin candidate for mid-Tyrone was returned on a simple and unambiguous platform: 'I believe in the use of force ... the more, the better'. At no point in the 1950s and 1960s did the hard-core republican vote in the Six Counties fall below 70,000. Also, although the IRA had been forced to abandon its 1950s campaign, it had survived, albeit weakened and demoralised, and stood by ominously in the wings, awaiting the opportunity to strike again. Meanwhile, some of its members, learning from recent experience, sought to broaden its appeal by moving politically to the left and identifying with, articulating and exploiting popular grievances amongst northern Catholics.

Minority Grievances Still Persist

Moreover, though Stormont ministers had implemented Westminster's social welfare legislation with both enthusiasm and imagination, numerous minority grievances remained. Whilst unionist leaders constantly restated their commitment to British democratic ideals, they made little or no effort to root out those elements of injustice and unfairness which had disfigured political life in Northern Ireland since its foundation. For example, they made no attempt at fundamental reform to eliminate religious discrimination or to overhaul the State's security apparatus. Even in the 1960s, 'one man, one vote' had still not been introduced as the basis for the local government franchise. As a result, over one quarter of those then eligible to vote in Westminster and Stormont parliamentary elections had no such entitlement in council contests.

This represented a major political misjudgment by unionist leaders as it gave their party only a marginal advantage, but it provided the later Civil Rights movement with its most emotive slogan. For example, in Belfast, 28 percent of Catholic and 19 percent of Protestant adults had no local government vote; in Derry the equivalent figures were 22 percent and 19 percent respectively. This slight distortion was, of course, compounded by the continued gerrymandering of local authority electoral areas; parliamentary constituencies gave little cause for legitimate grievance. In the 1950s and 1960s, nationalists usually had control of just eleven of the seventy-three councils in the Six Counties; they were manipulated out of this position in a number of localities where they had a clear, sometimes substantial, majority of electors. In some urban areas, the boundaries had been redrawn since the early 1920s in order to preserve or achieve unionist ascendancy (e.g. Omagh in 1935, Derry in 1936, Armagh in 1946). The composition of Derry Corporation provides one of the most blatant examples of electoral impropriety. In 1966, 14,229 Catholic voters there returned eight city councillors, whilst 8,781 Protestants returned twelve.

Religious Discrimination

Religious discrimination in public and private employment was traditional in the Six Counties. Bernadette Devlin, a leading Civil Rights activist in the 1960s, described it as being only less serious on the Catholic side because there were fewer Catholic bosses and fewer local authorities to practise it. Whatever their political composition, council allocation of job contracts and, to a lesser extent, houses on a sectarian basis, was commonplace. In the 1950s, Catholics comprised 31.5 percent of the total workforce employed by local government (their proportionate share) but they held just 11.8 percent of non-manual posts. Overall, Northern Ireland had continued its steady progress towards a 'Protestant State'. In the 1960s, 94 percent of its higher grade civil servants were Protestant, 62 of its 68 judges, 85 percent of the members of its statutory boards and 88 percent of its regular police force (approximately 80 percent of its upper ranks). The part-time armed Special

Constabulary (B Specials) numbered 12,000 and was in effect a Protestant militia. In private employment, Catholics tended to occupy jobs low in the socio-economic scale, with little status and high relative unemployment, and to cluster in the bottom reaches of all classes. The incidence of discrimination, however, was lessened by the government's considerable success in attracting foreign investors. They were more likely to fill vacancies strictly on merit than local family businesses and by the early 1970s provided work for over half the North's factory labour force.

In the early 1970s the unemployment rate amongst northern Catholics was more than two-and-a-half times the Protestant level. In part, this disparity reflected the widespread pattern of religious discrimination in employment. Local courts proved unable to provide redress for individuals even in instances where sectarian bias was patent; at the time, a preference for those from one's own milieu, recruited through informal contacts such as family or friends, was commonplace throughout the United Kingdom. Short-sightedly the government failed to take the initiative to ensure a more balanced workforce. But other factors also contributed to the unemployment differential, including the continuing reluctance of nationalists fully to recognise the Belfast parliament and enter local public sector occupations. One Catholic QC who accepted a county court judgeship was publicly denounced as a 'Judas Iscariot' by a fellow-Nationalist MP.

Academics have suggested additional explanations. Some have argued that the larger average family size amongst northern Catholics increased in proportion to the attractions of claiming state benefit rather than obtaining work. In addition, three-fifths of them lived in peripheral westerly areas of the province where there were fewer job opportunities as against one-fifth of the Protestant population. Moreover, the level of educational attainment within the minority was relatively low. In the 1950s its numbers accounted for fewer than 25 percent of grammar school places and of students enrolled in higher education.

Electoral manipulation and discrimination in employment were not the only causes of minority discontent. The level of public grants to Catholic schools continued to provide a simmering sense of injustice. Due to the shortfall in departmental funding, the Catholic church itself spent an estimated £20 million on educational provision (for example, on building and maintaining property) between 1947 and 1968. Friction also arose over the government's response to church applications to build new grammar schools, the issue of boarding scholarships to Catholic pupils who might more cheaply have attended a neighbouring state school and the payment of national insurance contributions to teachers in voluntary institutions. Meanwhile nationalist alienation was reinforced by the persistent impasse over the status and finances of the Mater Hospital.

Furthermore, the continued existence of the Special Powers Act caused controversy, even though it (along with parallel emergency legislation in the South) had been undeniably effective during the recent IRA campaign. This apart, its provisions had rarely been utilised. Nonetheless, critics projected it as evidence that Northern Ireland was a police state. Certainly its application had not been without bias. From time to time it had led to extensive police searches of Catholic districts particularly, prolonged interrogation of suspects and wrongful arrest and this had prompted allegations of damage to property, harassment and religious repression. There is, however, some evidence that the security forces were beginning to show 'greater impartiality'; Eamon McCann quotes a nationalist senator describing the RUC in 1963 as 'a fine body of men doing a good job'. Overall, the worst excesses of sectarian discrimination in housing and regional policy and in public and private employment and the most striking examples of gerrymandering occurred in the west of the province. Already in the mid-1950s, British officials were warning Stormont ministers that 'the existence of serious and chronic unemployment' in Derry and Newry 'adds to the risk of political disturbance', particularly given the 'long tradition of political rancour and violence' in Northern Ireland. It was in these peripheral urban areas that 'the Troubles' of the next decade first erupted.

Brooke's failure to attempt far-reaching institutional reform and to take steps to eradicate discrimination was largely due to his continuing obsession with party unity. On occasion he calculated that it was preferable to take decisions which would damage the government (i.e. be perceived by opponents and observers as biased and unfair) rather than risk a split in the Unionist and Orange parties, which could potentially undermine Northern Ireland's constitutional position. He never attempted to become a truly national leader. With regard to the minority, his only strategy or hope was that social reform and economic progress alone would undermine its nationalist aspirations.

Meanwhile, he was under no pressure from Westminster to initiate the fundamental changes which were needed. London's approach to the Six Counties until the mid-1960s remained one of 'benign neglect'. The IRA campaign (1956-1962) was used by Stormont to justify inaction. It certainly made ministers more wary of divisive and controversial measures. In the late 1940s the southern government's anti-partition drive had had a similar effect. Though subsequently Belfast-Dublin relations improved, sources of friction still abounded, as much over symbols as issues of substance. Thus southern leaders had protested at the 'provocative' royal visit in 1951; earlier they had expressed irritation over a Dutch naval force disembarking at Derry, when the memory of William III was still 'very much alive' and frequently claimed that 'deep offence to national sentiment' was caused by Northern court convictions for persons displaying the Irish tricolour.

Overall, those who supported reform, aimed at replicating British standards of democracy in the Six Counties, received insufficient backing from the unionist leadership. The attempt in 1959 to broaden party membership by recruiting Catholics and adopting them as candidates consequently achieved no tangible results. The Orange Order, which was much scorned by many middle-class Protestants, was the major obstacle to change. Sir George Clark, Grand Master of the institution, stated tersely: 'It is difficult to see how a Catholic could be acceptable ... as a member ... or unconditionally support [the party's] ideas.'

Brooke indicated that whilst he did not oppose the proposal, it was not, in his view, practical politically. He noted privately: 'There is no indication from either the nationalists or the church that they agree with us on the general policy of maintenance of the Constitution but they may come in later ... speeches will only delay matters.' His public statements were less restrained. He declared that there would be 'no change in the fundamental character of the Unionist Party ... If that is called inflexible then it shows that our principles are not elastic.'

A Dualistic Society

A Quaker survey into Northern Ireland, conducted during 1959-1962, concluded that though the area was 'stable' it remained 'deeply divided'. It recommended, as a matter of urgency, that both traditions 'learn more of the other's beliefs'. The dualistic nature of Ulster society evident in the inter-war years had deep historic roots and clearly still persisted. At the time of the report, 98 percent of Catholic primary school children attended exclusively Catholic schools. Then as now, teacher training was provided on a rigidly sectarian basis. Whilst 78 percent of university students claimed to have friendships across the religious divide, 96 percent rejected entering mixed marriages on principle; such marriages remained a rare phenomenon and almost inevitably generated bitterness and hostility. Outside the opulent middle-class suburbs, residential segregation by religious identity was almost complete. This all-embracing pattern of social exclusivity bred mutual ignorance, which in turn fostered prejudice.

The Quaker study commented on the 'cold war' which existed between the Protestant and Catholic churches where the attendance rate was 55 percent among Protestants and over 90 percent for the minority, one of the highest levels in Europe. It was also struck by the strong tendency for each 'to think the worst of the other side'. Even in the 1950s and early 1960s violent sectarian clashes were not unknown and, in keeping with tradition, usually originated in some ritual demonstration or commemorative march. Atavistic tribal hatreds remained latent and powerful, lurking not far beneath the surface. Some contemporaries were optimistic about the future, convinced that after the forty years since partition the two communities were at last learning to live together and that a better future for both was in prospect. Certainly, fundamental reform was urgently required and was bound to be hazardous and test to the full the uncertain skills of the Stormont leadership. It could well threaten the stability of a state so lacking in political consensus. Hardline republicanism had retained substantial core support, whilst elements within the IRA eagerly awaited any favourable opportunity to strike.

At the same time, an influential section within unionism would oppose any change which might dilute or weaken the Protestant ascendancy. Resolutions introduced at the party's annual conference suggest that a siege mentality and insecurity still persisted, despite the declaratory clause in the Ireland Act. Amongst these were proposals that 'too many non-unionists [were] buying property', Catholics were 'adopting too many children' and family allowances were being made available too indiscriminately. These are symptomatic of a deep-seated fear within the movement that, partly for demographic reasons, time was not on the side of the Union. Just after the war, Herbert Morrison had suggested to Brooke that 'owing to the higher [Catholic] birth rate ... our population would in the end defeat us.' He replied that 'it would not affect the situation in our lifetime'. By the early 1960s, when Brooke was over seventy years of age, 35 percent of Northern Ireland's population and 41 percent of its total school enrolment was Catholic. Given the marginal impact of the Stormont government's post-war reforms and policies on minority attitudes towards national unity, such figures were legitimate cause for continuing unionist anxiety.

O'Neill becomes Prime Minister

On 25 March 1963, ill-health, old age and mounting backbench criticism impelled Brooke reluctantly to resign as Prime Minister. After Lord Wakehurst, the Governor, had taken discreet soundings, Captain Terence O'Neill 'emerged' as head of government. His appointment owed more to aristocratic connections than evidence of political talent. Like Brooke, he was of Anglo-Irish landed background, claiming descent from the English Chichesters and the Celtic O'Neills of pre-British Ulster, once ancient kings of Ireland. His father was a Unionist politician, the first British MP to be killed in action during the First World War. In the tradition of his class, he spent his formative years outside Northern Ireland. He was brought up in his mother's liberal circle (she was the daughter of Lord Crewe, a member of Asquith's cabinet), educated at Eton, where he had been academically undistinguished, and later served with the Irish Guards in the Second World War, in which he reached the rank of Captain. He was arguably Brooke's natural successor. He had entered Stormont in 1946 (representing Bannside, 1946-1970), risen rapidly, serving at Home Affairs and then as Finance Minister for seven years (1956-1963) and deputising for the Premier during his absences and illnesses. Almost certainly, however, Brian Faulkner, the young (forty-two years old) mercurial and energetic Minister of Home Affairs (1959-1963), would have been the preference of Unionist MPs. He now became a dynamic Minister of Commerce, but an unreliable 'semi-detached' cabinet colleague.

Pressure for Reform

From the outset, O'Neill came under strong pressure to initiate fundamental internal reform. This stemmed not only from the increasingly assertive and confident minority, but also from the obvious need to compete with and outflank the Northern Ireland Labour Party (NILP); its recent electoral performance had given Unionists valid reason for concern. In due course, Harold Wilson's Labour government at Westminster (1964-1970) also urged the need for change. It had considerable leverage; Britain's net capital transfer to the Six Counties had reached over £70 million by 1968. The scope for political innovation in Ireland had earlier been widened by the appointment of Seán Lemass as Taoiseach of the Irish Republic (1959-1966). He was genuinely anxious to break once and for all the sterile 'cold war' mould of North-South relations since partition and to foster co-operation in matters of mutual interest, hoping thereby to hasten unity. He was Fianna Fáil's earliest and strongest proponent of this strategy.

For his part, O'Neill seemed conscious of both his responsibilities as leader and the opportunities fate had afforded him. Aged forty-eight, he was too young to remember 'the Troubles' of the early 1920s, which had conditioned the mind-set of his three predecessors. Days after taking office, he declared that 'our task' was 'to transform the face of Ulster with bold and imaginative measures'. Later, he was more specific, stating his intention to 'make Northern Ireland economically stronger and more prosperous ... and to build bridges between the two traditions within our community'. The achievement of these laudable, necessary but daunting objectives was made no easier by lingering uncertainty regarding the depth of his own personal commitment to the reforms which were required. Unlike some leading unionists, he had not publicly indicated his support for Catholic membership of the party during the bitter internal debate in 1959. Douglas Harkness, who was the leading civil servant in his department (Finance) then, states 'Close association with him ... never caused me to regard him as a liberal and ... he showed little of his later enthusiasm for Éire.' Harkness adds that later, as Premier, there was 'no relationship between [his] words ... and [his] actions' and that he saw himself as the 'brilliant, young, enthusiastic' John F Kennedy to the 'effete, worn-out Eisenhower' of Brooke.

Some historians consider that in office O'Neill's preoccupation was 'stealing Labour's thunder' (his own phrase) rather than allaying Catholic resentments. He certainly sought to expand and modernise the economy. But, though he used the rhetoric of conciliation (Kennedy's politics of expectation), he ultimately hoped that nationalist grievances would be dissolved by their shared participation in the benefits of growth. A contented, tolerant society would therefore emerge through advances in wealth, education and maturity, without any need for far-reaching structural reform. On this interpretation, his approach was similar to Brooke's – to make 'Ulster ... so prosperous that the traditional political barriers are broken down' – only more openly expressed and more systematically pursued.

Other commentators disagree: they are convinced that he had a genuine commitment to reform and sought to drag Northern Ireland into the twentieth century by transforming it into a fully democratic and just state. In short, they assert that he was the first Northern premier to make religious equality and the reconciliation of the minority an absolute priority of government policy. Whatever his intentions, his prospects of success were diminished by his limited political skills, personal aloofness, arrogant, patrician manner and condescending tones. 'If you treat Roman Catholics with due consideration and kindness,' he said, 'they will live like Protestants in spite of the authoritarian nature of their church.' His actions in government were the catalyst which brought Northern Ireland within six years to the brink of civil war. They failed to satisfy those seeking change but were sufficient to alarm reactionary elements within his own party.

CHAPTER 8

Agitation for Civil Rights

O'Neill's efforts to modernise the economy met with some success. During his premiership, Northern Ireland's total output of industrial production grew faster than that of the United Kingdom as a whole. Central government planning (more informed by expert advice than was usual at Stormont), heavy public expenditure and success in attracting foreign investment resulted in considerable expansion and diversification. Amongst the new firms to locate in the Six Counties were Goodyear, Michelin, Du Pont, Enkalon, ICI and Courtaulds. The growing output of synthetic fibres from factories, based mainly in east Antrim and Derry, was symbolic of the new era and these fibres seemed the natural replacement for linen textiles. A total of 30,000 new jobs was created. By 1973, over half the local labour force was employed in externally-owned firms, compared with one-third in the Republic.

Unfortunately, this impressive advance was largely offset by continued contraction in the North's narrow range of traditional manufactures; the government had been advised that the trend was irreversible. The production of linen, the region's oldest, most distinctive and internationally renowned industry, had virtually disappeared by the late 1950s. Massive redundancies affected ship-building from the early 1960s. Heavy public subsidies alone enabled it to escape closure, the common fate of most British yards. Traditional engineering firms likewise wilted in the face of foreign competition. Overall, between 1963 and 1969, the net increase in the manufacturing labour force was just

5,000 while the proportion of output from the more Catholic area west of the Bann rose from 17 percent to 23 percent between 1959 and 1971.

These structural changes in the economy had political repercussions. The many long-established family businesses, now entering terminal decline, had in the past formed part of the backbone of Ulster Unionism and had employed a mainly Protestant workforce. Their closure caused disillusion and resentment. The need to respond and to reassure influenced the content of O'Neill's other initiatives. A 'new city' (Craigavon) to house Belfast's overflow was constructed at Lurgan/Portadown, both Protestant towns, and a new university was sited at Coleraine, also a Protestant town (rather than at the predominantly Catholic Derry). These decisions reflected the Prime Minister's concern to placate, in particular, his party's working class supporters.

Reconciling the Minority

But there is also evidence – more in gesture than in substance – of O'Neill's concern to reconcile the minority. In mid-1963, he sent a message of condolence to Cardinal Conway on the occasion of Pope John XXIII's death. Flags at Belfast's City Hall were flown at half-mast as a mark of respect. Ian Paisley's first significant political act was to lead a demonstration in protest – the first-ever loyalist march to be banned under the Special Powers Act. Undeterred, the Prime Minister sought to build bridges across the inter-community divide through speeches attacking sectarianism and discrimination and visits to Catholic schools during 'meet the people' tours. He and his cabinet considered local government reform but hesitated due to fears of internal party opposition.

His most daring initiative was his meeting with Seán Lemass at Stormont in January 1965, the first between northern and southern leaders since the Boundary Agreement exactly forty years before. The secrecy surrounding the visit was such that neither his cabinet in Belfast nor the Home Office was informed until the day the Taoiseach (Prime Minister) arrived. Though the lack of preliminary consultation irritated some ministers, they later approved his actions. Even the staunchly unionist *Newsletter* described critics as 'irrational voices crying in the wilderness'. During the forty minutes of joint discussions, divisive constitutional issues were studiously avoided but increased co-operation in matters of mutual concern were examined. The co-ordination of tourism and electricity supplies was the most tangible result. O'Neill's reciprocal visit to Dublin in February was also regarded as a success by both politicians.

Grounds for Optimism

In 1969, a southern newspaper nominated O'Neill 'Irishman of the year'. Meanwhile at home, he had some grounds for believing that his efforts 'to break Northern Ireland out of the chain of fear which had bound her for forty-three years' were bearing fruit. In the November 1965 Stormont election, his party won 59.1 percent of the votes cast, its second-best result since 1921. During the contest, he had canvassed Catholic voters and what gratified him most was that he achieved what he described as the 'practical annihilation' of the Labour Party, winning back Protestant working-class voters from the socialist camp. Another outcome was that, in 1965, the Nationalist Party accepted for the first time the role of official opposition at Stormont, whilst retaining much of the anti-partitionist rhetoric which its supporters expected from it.

There is evidence, even at the end of the decade, that O'Neill held on to much popular support. When, in his December 1968 'Ulster at the crossroads' speech, he appealed for backing on television, he received 150,000 letters and telegrams and 120,000 newspaper coupons in sympathy. A public opinion survey conducted in 1968-1969 concluded that two-thirds of the minority believed community relations had improved since 1963. Since the war, the level of political guidance proffered by northern priests had diminished; this had facilitated a more independent and considered perspective on public life to develop within their congregations. The expanding Catholic middle class especially favoured the general direction of O'Neill's policies. However much they might aspire ultimately to unity, they were increasingly determined to acquire and to exercise full and equal political and civil rights within the Six Counties as their priority.

Meanwhile, physical force nationalism was at a low ebb. The IRA had little support. It suffered from defeatism and factionalism. Its traditionalists retained their republican creed and their Catholicism intact and, as in the past, awaited the opportunity to renew the armed struggle. They regarded as divisive and as a dangerous distraction those members more receptive to Marxist ideology, who were anxious to immerse themselves in popular agitation and to arouse sympathy for a future violent campaign.

Nonetheless, by the mid-1960s, Northern Ireland's slide towards ultimate ungovernability was already gathering momentum. A succession of emotive anniversaries provided the immediate context. In 1963,

121

Wolfe Tone Societies were formed to commemorate the bi-centenary of the revolutionary's birth and to remind the new generation of an old faith. They were to play a decisive role in destabilising the North before the end of the decade. The year 1966 likewise had a deep historical resonance throughout Ireland. It was the fiftieth anniversary of the Battle of the Somme – not a context conducive even to O'Neill's vacuous reform programme. It was also fifty years since the Easter Rising. In Dublin, Lemass's government was the foremost casualty of the changed atmosphere. His political realism foundered in a recrudescence of Irish irredentism and predictable electoral defeat. The Stormont government was sufficiently alarmed by these developments and the presumed threat of southern invasion that it temporarily closed a number of border roads.

Meanwhile, celebrations of these long-past but too well remembered events had sparked off riots in Belfast. More ominously, they had led to the first random murders of Catholics (at Malvern Street) by Protestant extremists in the most recent 'Troubles'. The assassins were members of the UVF; the force was promptly banned by O'Neill, who described it as this 'evil thing in our midst'.

Opposition to O'Neill builds

By 1966, O'Neill's leadership had already begun to generate powerful opposition within his own party. His greatest failure was his inability to bring its members with him. Inside the cabinet, Brian Faulkner indicated growing discomfiture at the broad thrust of policy. Arguably his criticisms owed as much to political rivalry and personal hostility as to disagreement on issues of principle. There were other more grave sources of discontent. Those sections of the Protestant working class employed hitherto in the North's traditional industries felt particular bitterness towards the Prime Minister, blaming him for their own relative economic decline and steadily contracting job prospects.

The most virulent hostility, however, came from elements within the Orange Order and the grass-roots unionist membership; those who, in O'Neill's opinion, regarded 'moderation as treason and decency as weakness'. They shared a deepening conviction that he was 'going too far', especially in considering local government reform, and that his often sudden policy initiatives and gestures posed a real threat to the Protestant ascendancy in the North and therefore the Union itself. They believed that he was betraying his and their religious and political heritage. No-one voiced their unease or exploited their fears more effectively than Dr Ian Paisley. In 1966, he launched a 'strategy of tension', expressly to arouse and articulate loyalist discontent.

Ian Paisley

Paisley was born in Armagh in 1926; his father was an independent Baptist preacher. He became self-styled moderator of his own Free Presbyterian Church, a sect which he formed in 1951 (its central citadel became the Martyrs' Memorial Church in Belfast). Several years later, he emerged as the leading figure in Ulster Protestant Action, a group established in response to the IRA campaign and dedicated to preserving Protestant dominance and values inside the Six Counties. In the mid-1960s it eventually mutated into his first political party, the Protestant Ulster Party, later renamed the Democratic Unionist Party (DUP).

Paisley combined fervent anti-Catholic bigotry and

intense evangelical Protestantism with inflammatory, bellicose rhetoric. He consistently claimed that O'Neill was a treacherous 'Lundy', a closet anti-unionist cravenly 'selling out' his own people. He also portrayed him along with numerous other liberals, modernisers and secularisers as an unwitting pawn in a nefarious conspiracy, hatched and orchestrated by the papacy. He roundly condemned all 'weakness' towards Rome the 'anti-Christ' and all symptoms of the 'Romeward trend'. In this he included all measures to ensure complete equality for Catholics (in jobs, housing and political life), any steps to improve relations with the South and also the ecumenism, then fashionable, of the World Council of Churches. He led the extra-parliamentary wing of unionism, thrived on street confrontation, in particular the counter-march or demonstration, and kept his followers on the streets through much of the 1960s.

O'Neill likened Paisleyism to fascism, citing their shared contempt for authority, crude intolerance, emphasis on monster rallies and processions, perverted patriotism and use of 'the sordid techniques of gangsters'. The comparison drew additional validity from Paisley's involvement, albeit obscure, in the revival of loyalist paramilitaries. In the mid-1960s he set up the Ulster Protestant Volunteers for Protestants of Ulster birth. Its function – to maintain the Protestant ascendancy – was encapsulated in its motto 'For God and Ulster'. It not only provided the shock troops for his counter-demonstrations but also acquired arms and bombed public utilities, hoping to incriminate the IRA as part of an elaborate ruse to discredit O'Neill. (The RUC even uncovered a plot to assassinate the Prime Minister.) Some of its members proceeded to revive the UVF which had been dormant for over forty years.

Few individuals did more than Paisley to reinstate the gun in local politics or to foment violent clashes in the province's streets. His widely-publicised actions provoked sectarian riots, fuelled the process of community polarisation and helped unleash the political extremism and tribalism always latent in Northern Ireland. They also resulted in his imprisonment and martyrdom (in 1966) shortly after he had launched his 'O'Neill must go, O'Neill will go' campaign. He began his doctoral thesis on St Paul in Crumlin Road jail. A contemporary survey estimated that he had by then the support of 14 percent of the adult population of the Six Counties. In hindsight it is clear that, partly due to his efforts, the old seemingly monolithic Unionist Party had begun to fragment. At the time it was evident that O'Neill would have to tread with extreme caution if he wished to translate his gestures of reconciliation into tangible reform measures.

Growing Minority Impatience

By the mid-1960s, the lack of substance behind O'Neill's rhetoric was causing mounting suspicion and criticism within the minority, especially among sections of its vociferous middle class. From the outset, the suddenness of his espousal of liberal policies had raised doubts regarding the genuineness of his commitment to reform. These were reinforced by some of his subsequent decisions. In particular, the siting of the North's second university at Coleraine and of a new city at Craigavon prompted allegations that the more Catholic areas west of the River Bann were being neglected. Even the name 'Craigavon', like that of Belfast's new 'Queen Elizabeth Bridge', suggested a continuing Protestant exclusivism.

Meanwhile, the major nationalist grievances – refusal

of 'one man, one vote' in local government elections, gerrymandering and sectarian discrimination – had been ignored. The traditional Stormont unwillingness to appoint a fair proportion of Catholics to public boards still persisted. No attempt had been made to broaden the membership of the Unionist Party. O'Neill himself remained an active member of the Orange Order, even joining its senior branch, the Royal Black Institution, in 1964. Moreover, the likelihood that he would ever of his own volition deliver significant reform appeared to be receding, given the intense pressures being applied by reactionary forces within his own party.

The Formation of Pressure Groups

In these circumstances, extra-parliamentary pressure groups in favour of change began to emerge. They were throughout predominantly Catholic and, at first, exclusively middle class. Their initial purpose was to raise awareness of inequality and pressurise O'Neill into conceding fundamental reforms. Later their objectives broadened and became more controversial; certainly they included a concern to rouse the minority out of the passivity which had generally characterised its political responses from the early 1920s.

The first such group to emerge was the Campaign for Social Justice (CSJ). It was comprised of thirteen Catholic professional people, galvanised into action in 1965 by the refusal of Dungannon Council, County Tyrone, to rehouse Catholics from an overcrowded estate into better-quality, post-war unoccupied dwellings. It proceeded to collect and publicise evidence of alleged sectarian discrimination (in housing and employment) and of unfair electoral practices (including gerrymandering and the failure to introduce 'one man, one vote'). It sought to obtain redress by bringing individual cases before the Northern Ireland courts (without success) and by seeking to influence opinion in Britain. It ignored issues which were perceived to be more specifically republican, such as the operation of the Special Powers Act and reform of the security forces. Likewise it steered clear of constitutional matters and strove to avoid any involvement in party politics. It had little or no impact beyond the educated and concerned section of its own community.

The Northern Ireland Civil Rights Association (NI-CRA), founded on 9 April 1967, eventually proved to be by far the most important of the pressure groups formed in this period. Its foundation was a symptom of the widespread impatience and frustration caused by the glacial pace of reform at Stormont as well as the ineffectiveness of the CSJ. It was influenced by the use of direct action, especially in the United States, to effect change. This was the first significant occasion in which global trends impinged on regional politics. It focused attention on the same largely Catholic grievances as the CSJ but, whilst it too avoided the partition question, it campaigned on a wider spectrum of issues. These included the repeal of the Special Powers Act and the disbandment of the B Specials.

The organisation was distinguished by its broadly representative membership. Its founders were drawn from seven different political parties (including the Nationalist, Communist, Liberal, Labour and even Young Unionist) and, in addition, academics, trade unionists and republicans. It was therefore unique in the history of the Six Counties. At the outset, probably most of those involved aimed to create a strong, non-sectarian mass movement, committed to the attainment of full political and civil rights for all. They believed that, if successful, reform would come quickly. This was never a likely scenario. NICRA remained throughout a predominantly Catholic movement. Also given the political traditions of the North and the government's responsiveness to its ultra-conservative grass roots, rapid progress was an unrealistic expectation.

Role of Republicans in NICRA

A minority amongst the movement's founders – the republicans – worked to a different agenda. Though not in control of NICRA until 1970, they nonetheless played a formative role in its development. According to Gerry Adams, current president of Sinn Féin, 'the republicans were in the movement ... from the beginning'. The idea of a civil rights agitation was first mooted at a Wolfe Tone Society's conference in August 1966. The proposal was made by members of the Dublin branch, then in effect an IRA debating society, with the full support of Cathal Goulding and other leading figures within the force. Republicans were well-represented on the NICRA executive committee, set up nine months later. Thirty of the eighty persons present at the movement's first annual meeting (February 1968) were IRA activists. Though most of these remained committed to the need for force to achieve Irish unity ('Brits out'), they saw advantages in identification with an open protest movement. In part, they regarded it as a means of attracting increased popular backing for the republican cause.

Learning the lessons of the 1950s campaign, they perceived this to be a necessary pre-condition for the successful renewal of the armed struggle. The stirrings

Ulster Unionist Council, chaired by Sir Edward Carson, finalising preparations
Covenant Day, at the Ulster Hall, Belfast, 23 September 1912. *(The Graphic)*

Sir Edward Carson inspects a unit of the Ulster Volunteer Force, at Balmoral, Belfast, 6 June 1914. At the time, civil war in Ireland over the issue of Irish self-government seemed unavoidable.
(Linen Hall Library)

Northern Ireland's first cabinet, appointed May 1921 – (left to right)
E M Archdale, Sir R Dawson Bates, 7th Marquis of Londonderry, Sir J Craig (Prime Minister), H McD Pollock and J M Andrews.
(Public Record Office of Northern Ireland)

...ldiers leaving for the front, 10 November 1939. (Bigger Collection)

...merican troops disembark at Belfast Docks, 26 January 1942; these were the ...t GIs to set foot in Europe during the Second World War. *(Belfast Telegraph)*

Sean Lemass, Taoiseach, meeting Captain Terence O'Neill, northern Premier, at the entrance to Stormont Castle, Belfast, 14 January 1965. The respective heads of the two states had not met since December 1925. (Public Record Office of Northern Ireland)

republican suspect being interned by troops in the Markets area of Belfast, 1 August 1971. *(Belfast Telegraph)*

ishop Daly of Derry leads an injured man towards safety during 'Bloody Sunday', 0 January 1972, when thirteen civilians were shot dead by members of the st Parachute Regiment. (Pacemaker)

Agreement is reached on the setting up of the only joint unionist/-nationalist cabinet in Northern Ireland's history, at Sunningdale, Berkshire, 9 December 1973 – (left to right) Oliver Napier (Alliance Party leader), Liam Cosgrave (Taoiseach), Edward Heath (British Prime Minister), Brian Faulkner (Unionist leader) and Gerry Fitt (northern Nationalist leader). *(Belfast Telegraph)*

The funeral of Bobby Sands leaves Twinbrook for the republican plot at Millfield Cemetery, Belfast. Sands died on 5 May 1981, after a 66-day hunger strike at the Maze prison – the first of ten republican prisoners to die in support of their demand for political status. *(The Irish Times)*

Gerry Adams and Martin McGuinness during the Sinn Féin conference at Letterkenny, Co Donegal, 23/24 July 1994, at which motions critical of the Downing Street Declaration were passed, dampening hopes of an IRA ceasefire. (Pacemaker)

John Major with Patrick Mayhew at Stormont Castle, Belfast, 16 September 1994. He was appealing for loyalists to call a cease-fire, and for a clearer indication from the IRA that their campaign was over permanently. (Pacemaker)

Republican mural which appeared in mid-1994, urging British withdrawal from Northern Ireland. The 'TIME TO GO' slogan was first coined by left-wing Labour party activists in Britain, June 1988. (Pacemaker)

of northern Catholic resentment at the slow pace of change were perceived by them as an unmissable opportunity to promote their own political fortunes. But they hoped that other benefits would flow from their participation. An effective mass agitation might compel O'Neill to make concessions which would split his cabinet and party and undermine his government, so opening up the opportunity for the more effective use of force. It could at least cause northern ministers to lift their ban on republican clubs, on Sinn Féin and on publications such as *The United Irishman*, so facilitating future propaganda. Finally, republican involvement might also arrest the recent high turnover in IRA recruits by providing an alternative outlet for the energies of those frustrated by the lack of physical force activity.

In mid-1968, NICRA took the fateful decision to organise street demonstrations in Northern Ireland. The arguments in favour appeared to be overwhelming. Little or nothing had been achieved during the first eighteen months of the association's existence – the government had failed to investigate its complaints (William Craig, Minister of Home Affairs, 1966-1968, was particularly unresponsive), morale was flagging and meetings of its executive were ill-attended. At the same time, members were impressed and encouraged by the aggressive, sometimes successful, methods of international protest movements – in the United States, at the London School of Economics and at the Sorbonne in Paris. It was felt that such an approach, applied locally, might at last fully mobilise latent discontent and shake the Unionist leadership out of its apparent indifference and lethargy.

A broad consensus of NICRA members, from mid-dle-class members of the CSJ to committed republicans, favoured the change of tactics. A later Westminster inquiry was to condemn the 'failure in leadership and foresight' shown by all sides throughout this period. Certainly from the outset, there were obvious risks that public demonstrations would result in clashes with loyalists and police. Whatever their intention, it was likely that peaceful, non-political protesters would attract, and possibly be outnumbered by, those who were less cautious, more extreme, bent not on reform but on confrontation and ultimately on destabilising and overthrowing the Six Counties. In retrospect, the marches proved to be a catalyst. They rapidly passed out of the control of the original NICRA executive and led within months to the disintegration of the North's fragile political stability. Hooligans, Paisleyites, revolutionaries, the police and the government largely determined the pattern and flow of events in the streets.

The March to Dungannon

The first NICRA-sponsored march took place between Coalisland and Dungannon on 24 August 1968. It was a protest against sectarian bias in local housing allocation (the worst excesses in religious discrimination were concentrated in the area west of the Bann). It was provoked specifically by the eviction of a Catholic family who had squatted in a council house, which was then offered to a nineteen-year-old, single Protestant woman, previously the secretary of a unionist parliamentary candidate. The protest was organised by Austin Currie, then Nationalist MP for East Tyrone, aided by two nationalist councillors and three republicans. Two thousand people attended. They were marshalled by seventy stewards provided by the IRA; most of the volunteers in its northern units were present. No weapons, banners or symbols were carried but republican songs were sung and a last minute attempt by the IRA to appeal from the platform for support was narrowly averted by Fred Heatley, a moderate member of the Association's executive. Police succeeded in preventing a potentially serious clash with a loyalist counter-demonstration, arranged by Ian Paisley.

The Derry March

Heartened by this successful, peaceful and widely publicised protest, NICRA backed a second march – in Derry – on 5 October 1968. (The 'maiden city', rather than Belfast, was at the cutting edge of political events up to August 1969). The march was organised by small, fringe left-wing groups, in particular the neo-Marxist Derry Housing Action Committee. According to Eamon McCann, one of its members, their intention was 'to provoke the police into over-reaction and so spark off mass reaction against the authorities'. From the outset, Eddie McAteer, the Glagow-born Nationalist Party leader and MP for Foyle, felt uneasy 'at the company [NICRA] ... was keeping': he had to be dissuaded from withdrawing. Meanwhile, the demonstration was banned by government order after local loyalists (Apprentice Boys) once again provocatively called a counter-march to coincide with the Association's plans. But on 4 October, the NICRA leadership accepted McCann's view: 'We are marching and that's that.' Their agreed route led through Derry's walled inner city – a destination 'unheard of' (McCann) for such a protest. When next day, their progress was blocked by the RUC, fierce rioting erupted between police and marchers. (RTE's film of police batoning was televised throughout the world). McAteer and Gerry Fitt were among the

injured, rioting spilled inevitably into the Catholic Bogside and, before finally subsiding, over eighty people
had been hurt.

The clash was a milestone in the disintegration of
Northern Ireland's political life and its transfer to the
streets. Earlier signs of increasing tolerance and of
progress towards stability were thrown dramatically
into reverse. Ancient hatreds were rekindled, the two
communities progressively polarised. Those striving for
a better, fuller democracy were overwhelmed by a
revival of tribal loyalties and bitterness. The minority
was incensed by the perceived image of mainly Protestant security forces brutally suppressing those coura-
geously championing its most basic political and civil
rights. The Nationalist Party withdrew from Stormont in
protest and belatedly identified with NICRA's agenda.
John Hume, a little-known teacher, now built up his
reputation as a campaigner and vice-chairman of Derry
Citizens' Action Committee; he displaced McAteer as
MP for Foyle in February 1969. Republican assertions
that Northern Ireland was a police state seemed to have
been amply demonstrated. Certainly, constabulary
training to deal with civilian protest was inadequate, its
tactics were crude and its discipline uncertain. Later
government inquiries concluded that the RUC was
seriously at fault on a number of occasions and inept,
but added that its members 'struggled manfully to do
their duty ... Their courage ... was beyond praise.'

The knee-jerk response of William Craig, minister
responsible for law and order, was utterly to discount
any suggestion that the civil rights agitation was concerned with achieving greater justice. He regarded it
exclusively as a republican front, whose aim was to
foment disorder in preparation for a new IRA campaign.
Such hostile attitudes on the part of the authorities

contributed to the transformation of NICRA, both in its numerical support and its character. The impact of the October violence upon its fortunes was astonishing. Beforehand, it had been a small, isolated, ineffective and frustrated group; within weeks it mushroomed into a mass movement with a branch in most Catholic towns. Its subsequent marches, to Derry and Armagh, on 16 and 30 November 1968, each attracted 15,000 protesters, conspicuously defying the efforts of both loyalists and police to drive them off the streets. The Association changed dramatically, not only in scale but in leadership. By early 1969, many of its founding members had withdrawn or had been swept aside: young, militant, radical, Catholic working-class activists became predominant and set the tone of the movement.

A further symptom of accelerating political polarisation was the progressive withdrawal of liberal Protestants from NICRA. Their numbers in any case had never been large. Many unionists had been suspicious of the Association from its foundation, partly because of the involvement of known republicans, and they became ever more convinced from the autumn of 1968 that it was working to a republican agenda. They were also discouraged by its unwillingness to endorse unambiguously the Constitution of Northern Ireland. Moreover, they resented what they perceived as exclusive preoccupation with minority grievances and its implicit assumption that the majority was the sole source of all Ulster's ills. They noted, for example, its failure to criticise instances of Catholic discrimination against Protestants. Some civil rights activists were sensitive to this allegation. Describing a demonstration in Newry, Bernadette Devlin commented on the inconsistency of 'Catholic employers marching in protest against the Protestants they excluded from their factories'.

People's Democracy and Burntollet

Devlin herself first rose to prominence in the civil rights movement at Queen's University, Belfast, where she was studying psychology. In March 1969 she was elected to Westminster for mid-Ulster; she became the youngest woman ever returned to the Commons and the youngest MP for fifty years. The actions taken by the Queen's University students raised the political temperature still further. They began the new term on 9 October 1968 by forming People's Democracy (PD). Its members were young and radical. They ridiculed NICRA as right-wing and Catholic and were equally scathing of Jack Lynch's 'green Tory' Republic in the South. They were initially stirred to action by sympathy for the Derry marchers; some, like Devlin, had been there. They were animated especially by a sense of moral outrage at the action of the police and their primary demand was for an official enquiry and the repeal of the Special Powers Act.

Over the next three months PD branches were formed far beyond the campus and the movement's increasingly militant leadership began preparations for a 'long march', from Belfast to Derry, between 1-4 January 1969. The intention was to finish on the route planned by McCann and others, three months earlier, but blocked by the RUC. Moderate nationalist opinion in Derry advised against. So also did NICRA. Its members were feeling the strain of continuous activity on the streets and were anxious to divert more energy into building up the organisation. Also, O'Neill had appealed for a 'cooling-off' period (December 1968), had sacked William Craig and seemed intent on reform. In these circumstances the Association wished to show willingness to compromise.

The students were not dissuaded. On New Year's Day, about forty gathered at Belfast's City Hall to walk the seventy-five mile journey. By the time they had reached Burntollet Bridge on 4 January, seven miles from their final destination, their numbers had swollen to five hundred – most of them local people. There they were attacked by some two hundred loyalists armed with sticks and stones. Thirteen of the marchers required hospital treatment after the assault. Civil rights spokesmen later condemned the lack of protection provided for them by the eighty-strong police force in attendance. Their arrival in Derry was the signal for furious rioting in the Bogside, which was fuelled by further allegations of constabulary misconduct.

The Impact of Burntollet

The whole episode represented another watershed in Northern Ireland's drift towards civil war. Thereafter, every protest demonstration ended in violence. Elements within the IRA finalised plans to take the offensive against the security forces and exploit the embittered nationalist mood. During 1969, there were nine explosions and 73 shootings with 711 police and 22 military personnel injured and 13 people dead. It was the beginning of twenty-five years of the latest 'Troubles'. Meanwhile, hopes of compromise diminished as civil rights groups progressively hardened their demands to include the disarmament of the police, the abolition of the B Specials and the provision of jobs and houses.

Competition between the various bodies encouraged this trend. Above all, they were radicalised by bitter clashes with police and loyalists in the streets. Moreover, as the violence escalated, moderate leaders and students withdrew. Generally, young radicals, ideologically committed Marxists and republicans filled their places. The head of RUC Special Branch claimed that by May 1969 members of republican clubs controlled two-thirds of the executives of all local NICRA branches, that six of the fourteen members of the Association's executive were active in the republican movement and that the Citizens' Defence Committees, which had emerged in nationalist areas of Belfast, Derry, Newry, Lurgan and other towns, were IRA dominated.

Greater militancy was also encouraged by clear signs that both the Stormont government and Unionist Party were disintegrating and consequent rising hopes of forcing Westminster or Dublin to intervene. From October 1968, the British leadership did indeed apply increased pressure on O'Neill to speed up reform. But he hesitated, conscious of the dangers of a Protestant backlash. Civil rights concessions alarmed loyalists and fuelled their extremism, their hostility to change growing in proportion to nationalist expectations. Paisley's support reached new heights. He adroitly exploited unionist fears for the future of the Union. His earlier claims that the Prime Minister's policies would 'ruin Ulster' seemed vindicated. A subsequent Westminster inquiry into the origins of 'the Troubles' condemned his role in fanning the flames of sectarian distrust and violence.

On the Brink of Chaos

In December 1968, O'Neill despairingly attempted to seize the initiative. He dismissed Craig, his strongest right-wing critic, announced a programme of reforms and appeared on local television to appeal for support.

He stated with candour: 'We are on the brink of chaos ... neighbour could be set against neighbour.' He requested with limited success a halt to civil rights demonstrations and warned loyalists: 'If we do not face up to our problems, the Westminster parliament may act over our heads.'

Harold Wilson spoke of the unionist leader being 'blackmailed by thugs' and reaffirmed that, if he was overthrown, Northern Ireland's constitutional position would be reappraised.

Perhaps encouraged by the level of public sympathy after his media statement, O'Neill decided to go to the polls (his 'crossroads election') on 24 February 1969. The outcome weakened him beyond recovery. The Unionist Party split. It fielded both pro- and anti-O'Neill candidates; they received 173,805 and 95,696 votes respectively. Those in favour of reform did best in the moderate middle-class suburbs and least well in Protestant communities located close to areas of high Catholic concentration in Belfast and along the border. On 28 April, O'Neill resigned, leaving an insoluble legacy to his successor and cousin, Major Chichester-Clark. Paisley boasted that he had 'brought down a captain [O'Neill] and could bring down a major as well.'

Unionist Party Fragments

It was mainly the civil rights agitation which caused the Unionist Party to fragment. By the mid-1950s a minority of its members, drawn largely from the middle-class, favoured reform and modernisation. They were imbued with liberal ideals, regarded themselves as British and were genuinely eager to construct fully democratic institutions in Northern Ireland based on the Westminster model. Others, many of them working-class, fervently opposed change. They were traditionalist and majoritarian, determined to preserve Protestant power and to exclude Catholics from political influence. Primarily they identified with 'Ulster' rather than Britain. Leaders such as Brooke had been skilled in fudging sensitive issues. They accepted in principle the need for reform but procrastinated, arguing for gradualism in the interests of unity. This response was not open to O'Neill. NICRA forced its programme onto the Unionist Premier's agenda. He and his erstwhile supporters were compelled to choose between the application of liberal, democratic principles and the retention of one-party domination and the Protestant state. The British government added to the pressures. After forty years of 'benign neglect', it belatedly reinforced minority demands for full civil and political rights.

The Arrival of British Troops

By mid-1969, Stormont ministers had made important concessions. Derry Corporation had been replaced by a nine-member Development Commission, an ombudsman appointed to respond to complaints against government departments and steps taken to ensure that public housing was allocated on the basis of need. Reform of both local authority franchise and the Special Powers Act was under review. These measures, however, seemed to exacerbate rather than reduce the level of violence. During the summer of 1969 'marching season', politics and power moved decisively to the streets and Stormont ministers were reduced to impotence.

Derry once again set the pace. In April, it was already in a state of anarchy; after clashes between civil rights supporters and Paisleyites on 19 and 20 April, 160 casualties, over half of them members of the constabulary, needed hospital treatment. In the Bogside, Samuel Devenney died due, nationalists claimed, to the brutality of the police. They came to regard him as 'the first martyr of the troubles'. Chichester-Clark's appointment as premier brought a brief respite. But the Orange demonstrations, held on Monday, 13 July, sparked off further furious rioting in the city and to a lesser extent elsewhere. It erupted once more with even greater intensity when the Apprentice Boys held their annual march on 12 August. A cataclysmic Catholic/police confrontation – the notorious 'Battle of the Bogside' – ensued. To divert the authorities, prevent constabulary reinforcements being drafted in and perhaps foment a crisis, nationalists attacked local RUC stations throughout the Six Counties – at Coalisland, Strabane, Newry, Lurgan, Dungiven, Enniskillen and west Belfast.

Eventually, with the security forces overstretched and facing exhaustion, Chichester-Clark had no choice but to request that the British army intervene. James Callaghan (Home Secretary 1967-1970) gave permission and the troops were deployed on 14 August. As Derry eased, Belfast tensed. During the summer of 1969, 1,826 families were driven from their homes in the city, over 1,500 of them Catholic. In the course of two days, 14/15 August, sectarian clashes left seven people dead and 750 injured. On 14 August, the first IRA shots of the renewed 'Troubles' were heard on Cupar Street. Next day, a fifteen-year-old Fianna youth, Gerald McAluley, was shot dead by a Protestant mob in an attack on Bombay Street off the Falls Road. The Provisional IRA honour him as 'the first volunteer to die'. At 4.30 on that morning, British troops were already in the process of moving into neighbouring streets on the request of Harold Wolseley, RUC Police Commissioner.

Emergence of the Provisionals

Two factors precipitated the birth of the Provisionals in the autumn of 1969. Firstly, the explosion of violence in Belfast, especially during July/August, undermined the credibility of the old IRA. It had then no more than sixty volunteers in the city and just thirteen guns. It proved incapable of protecting Catholic areas and had done so little that was visible during the midsummer crisis that the slogan 'IRA – I Ran Away' was soon afterwards daubed on gable walls in Catholic areas.

Republicans were particularly outraged by the resulting welcome given to the British army; the mood was so relaxed that soldiers drinking in Falls Road pubs left their rifles on the bar counter when going to relieve themselves. At the same time, the sectarian assault which the minority had experienced created in a few days an atmosphere in which armed rebellion against the State could prosper. By the year's end, the PIRA had been formed (the title 'provisional' drawn from the Easter Rising proclamation), with forty-one-year-old London-born Seán MacStiofáin as Chief of Staff. It represented a reassertion of traditional republicanism – the use of force to drive the 'Brits out' and establish a thirty-two county Irish Republic. In highly favourable circumstances it attracted not only young recruits but many veterans of former IRA campaigns. Within six months its strength was believed to be around 1,500 throughout Ireland, including 800 in the North (600 in Belfast, 100 in Derry).

Twenty-one years earlier in November 1948, during the anti-partition campaign, when the South became a Republic, Lord Rugby, the then British Ambassador in Dublin, had warned unionists 'it will be a day of triumph for Éire if the forces of the Crown are actively employed against patriotic elements in Ireland. British bayonets are Ireland's secret weapon.' Certainly, Westminster's direct involvement in northern security after its troops were deployed in August 1969 was a major step towards its later decision in March 1972 to suspend the Stormont government altogether.

CHAPTER 9

'The Troubles'

Westminster's decision to deploy troops in Derry and in Belfast concluded fifty years of 'benign neglect' but did not end its relative ignorance of the Six Counties. The area generally remained a low priority on Britain's political agenda. The initial strategy adopted by British ministers was to use the army to patrol the streets and to attempt to keep the warring factions apart. By 10 September 1969 it had completed a 'peace line' – originally a makeshift barrier erected to separate the Catholic Falls from the Protestant Shankill area of Belfast. (In 1982 it was replaced by a high brick wall which still survives.) At the same time, the army supervised a far-reaching reform programme devised in response to earlier civil rights demands and aimed at fully extending British standards of democracy to Northern Ireland. It was hoped that the minority would quickly become convinced of the equity of local institutions and come to accept continued unionist control. It was expected that order would thus be restored and the British military presence ended within one to two years. Direct rule from Westminster (and Stormont's abolition) was initially regarded as unnecessary. It was an option which it had, after all, successfully avoided for almost fifty years.

A flood of wide-ranging reforms followed quickly after the arrival of the troops. The much maligned B Special constabulary was disbanded. It was replaced by the Ulster Defence Regiment (UDR), which was placed under British army rather than police control. The RUC was itself disarmed and reorganised and a new reserve force and a new complaints procedure instituted. The local government franchise was at last amended to 'one man, one vote' and council powers were progressively and drastically contracted in order to eliminate religious discrimination and improve administrative efficiency. Public housing construction and allocation was likewise centralised for the same reasons and a ministry established to promote inter-communal understanding and toleration.

These initiatives coincided with, and helped stimulate, some encouraging developments. On 21 April 1970, the Alliance Party was founded with liberal, cross-community middle-class support. It was moderate and pro-reform – a conscious attempt to break the sectarian mould of Ulster politics. Exactly four months later, on 21 August, the Social Democratic and Labour Party (SDLP) was formed. This was a constitutional nationalist party, centre-left in outlook, whose youthful leadership for the first time sought to use the political system to promote minority interests. It was committed to unity by consent of a majority in the North. It gleaned support from civil rights activists, the labour movement and old nationalist party elements, and received much-needed financial backing from the Republic. Its founders hoped that it could focus Catholic discontent back on Stormont and shift it away from direct action on the streets.

The Provisionals Gather Strength

Britain's intervention prevented outright civil war but did not stop an escalation in vicious sectarian conflict. Reform satisfied some moderates but had little or no impact on young, working-class militants in the urban ghettos. By August 1969, the civil rights movement had unleashed forces beyond its founders' control and had itself become more extreme. Its most radical elements denied the possibility of reform and favoured over-throwing the northern 'police state' through street confrontation and alliance with revolutionary national-ism. Their actions together with the Stormont govern-ment's response and a rising Protestant sectarian backlash polarised opinion further; levels of violence rose and a truly revolutionary situation resulted. The RUC was too small a force and was inadequately trained to deal with such civil disorder and its reforms entirely failed to instil confidence amongst northern Catholics. Northern ministers, therefore, relied heavily on the British army. Its role was much greater than Westminster had hoped but it was unable to prevent increased rioting and initially treated the barricades, erected to control access to the Catholic Falls and Bogside, with caution – these remained 'no go' areas for the security forces.

The Provisional IRA ably exploited this favourable context. Its capability and organisation rapidly matured through the acquisition of arms and the formation of an Army Council, a newspaper *An Phoblacht,* the founding of a separate Sinn Féin and the setting up of a Belfast-based northern command. It had little interest in reform or civil rights. Its emergence represented a revival of an older nationalist faith – the physical force republicanism inspired by Wolfe Tone and Patrick Pearse. It has consistently been immune to compro-mise; though it combined nationalism, socialism and sectarianism, for the next twenty-five years its defining feature was its stark objective – 'Brits out' and the formation of an all-Ireland republic. This it sought to achieve by bringing death, casualties and destruction to British and Northern Irish streets and by making the Six Counties ungovernable and Britain's interest in them unprofitable by the brutal punishment of suspected informers and the skilful use of propaganda. It was, from the outset, socially representative of the minority. Events from the late 1960s had created a climate in which it could operate and in which it was thought to fulfil a necessary role. Many Catholics felt an instinctive sympathy for its interpretation of the North's history and contemporary politics and were willing to accept intimidation, racketeering and sectarian assassination as unavoidable evils in a just war. The Provisional leadership considered that their mandate derived ultimately not from the people but from the fact of a British presence on Irish soil. Their actions helped force a more confrontational response from a, by now, moderate Stormont government.

The first objective of PIRA was to turn northern nationalist opinion against the British army and so assume the leadership of the Catholic ghettos. This it achieved, assisted by civil rights militants, by provoking riots and focusing street violence on the troops; (the first military fatality was in February 1971). They, in turn, directed their activity towards Catholic areas. Their perceived over-reaction – their (illegal) imposition of a curfew on the lower Falls (July 1970), use of CS gas and firing of plastic bullets (August 1970) – rapidly antagonised local opinion, initially in west Belfast. Thereafter, not only in nationalist Ireland but beyond, the military presence was widely regarded as a repressive and imperialist force, the enemy of the people, upholding and imposing Stormont/Westminster rule. PIRA was widely perceived as the minority's legitimate protector. Despite severe security measures (mandatory prison sentences for rioting, the banning of all marches from 23 July 1970, etc), it was soon strong enough to move from defence and provocation to the offensive. In 1970 alone, twenty-five persons died due to political violence, there were 213 shooting incidents, over 150 bombs exploded (during 1969/70, the disturbances caused £5.5 million damage) and the trend was rising alarmingly. In June 1971, the British army GOC, Sir Harry Tuzo, was already suggesting that a permanent solution could not be achieved by military means.

A short-term objective of the emerging PIRA campaign was to compel intervention in the North by the Irish Republic. During 1969/70, the return of 'the Troubles' to the Six Counties precipitated the gravest political crisis in the South since the civil war almost fifty years earlier. It exposed deep fissures in Jack Lynch's Fianna Fáil government. Lynch felt sympathy for the minority and espoused the goal of Irish unity; the primary aim of the party he led was 'the unity and independence of Ireland as a republic' but he hesitated to become directly involved in Ulster's problems, either by sending arms or despatching troops across the border. A number of his statements were, however, ambiguous; in August, 1969, he commented 'we can't stand by and see innocent people killed or worse'. Some southern army units were deployed along the border, raising minority hopes and greatly alarming Stormont ministers. More committed republicans in the Dublin cabinet meanwhile went further, making speeches which overtly threatened military intervention. In late 1969, they covertly transferred to the North £80,000 to help nationalists there purchase arms. When informed of these events in the Dáil by the opposition leader, the Taoiseach promptly sacked the three ministers whom he held responsible. At the later 'Arms Trial', one of these, Charles Haughey, denied complicity but stated afterwards: 'I did what I thought was right in the best interests of the country.'

The Unionists Fragment

With greater success, the IRA campaign aimed to impel unionists into more extreme political positions and to provoke retaliatory violence, so damaging further Stormont's credibility, undermining its prospects of restoring peace and hopefully forcing Westminster to impose direct rule. The British government's reform programme also antagonised much unionist opinion whilst failing to dispel Catholic grievances. During the early seventies, the movement fragmented into five pro-Union parties. This division was caused by conflicting attitudes towards the liberalising measures being introduced and towards Westminster. These strains were aggravated by personality clashes and the contrasting class identity and religious preferences of unionist supporters. Militants regarded the civil rights groups as a threat to Protestant domination of Ulster and an IRA front. They saw reform as appeasement and they urged that 'disloyalists' be suppressed. By 1970, Paisley aimed to bring the Stormont government down on the grounds that it was destroying Ulster's 'Protestant heritage'. The context of violence, polarisation and uncertainty transformed him from a street politician on the margins of politics into a significant, province-wide, political force in all but nationalist areas. He entered Stormont in 1970, winning O'Neill's Bannside seat in a by-election and two months later stood successfully for the Westminster constituency of North Antrim. He and his party (called the Democratic Unionist Party from September 1971), were active, attuned to Protestant fears and expressed clear, if unobtainable, objectives. Their activities helped stall reforms, deepen sectarian division and fuel nationalist alienation.

The Loyalist Paramilitaries

Meanwhile, republican violence, the perceived ineffectiveness of the security forces and the reform programme all boosted loyalist paramilitary membership. The temporary disarming of the RUC and disbandment of the special constabulary caused serious rioting in the Belfast Shankill, a Protestant area, on 12 October 1969, during which Constable Victor Arbuckle died. He was the first RUC fatality in the current 'Troubles'. The UVF spread beyond its urban heartlands but remained small, illegal (from 1966) and secretive. In contrast, the Ulster Defence Association (UDA) reached a peak membership of 40,000 by 1972 and was legal (1972-1992). It had been formed two years earlier, when vigilante groups spontaneously emerged in Protestant working-class areas of Belfast to blockade streets as a defence against IRA sniping and bombing attacks; in 1971, these merged into units and brigades. It was throughout a self-consciously working-class movement and, at the outset at least, genuinely popular. It attracted then some respectable local figures – community leaders, trade unionists, ex-servicemen – who regarded themselves as decent, law-abiding citizens, driven reluctantly by circumstances to become soldiers. Nonetheless, the Protestant paramilitaries suffered from recruits of poor quality, motivated as much by thuggery as by patriotism. Their activities were never solely defensive; their violence was often spontaneous, incompetent and randomly sectarian, marked by the retaliatory bombing of public houses in nationalist areas or indiscriminate shooting of Catholics. In part, this was because targets which might be regarded as legitimate – Sinn Féin/PIRA members or their active supporters – were difficult to identify and often impossible to locate. The intention of the loyalist paramilitaries was to wreak revenge for republican violence, to pressurise the PIRA into abandoning its campaign and to communicate to the minority that there was a price to be paid even for passive support of Provisional activities. The intensification of the PIRA campaign pre-dated the increase in sectarian killings by Protestants. But these actions by the UVF/UDA damaged their morale and diminished their support; middle-class Protestants generally regarded them with contempt. In contrast, the PIRA attracted more skilled and competent volunteers, had a clear and coherent strategy and was in a position to choose from a wide range of identifiable and accessible targets which were perceived by sympathisers to be 'legitimate'. These included military and police personnel, civilians who furnished their needs within the community at large and both government property and commercial premises.

Internment – a Disastrous Mistake

Against the background of an escalating PIRA campaign and the retaliatory viciousness of the loyalist paramilitaries, the Stormont premier, Chichester-Clark, resigned on 20 March 1971. He could see 'no other way' to bring home 'the realities of the present constitutional, political and security situation'. Brian Faulkner was an obvious successor. He was fifty years old, an Orangeman but moderate and pragmatic as well as ambitious. He also had considerable experience – a successful businessman, who had entered the Commons, aged twenty-eight, in 1949, then the youngest MP in Stormont history, and had subsequently enjoyed a distinguished career. Now, as Premier, he immediately sought to heighten party unity, and broaden his government's appeal through his choice of cabinet and the formation of parliamentary committees, some chaired by the SDLP. But the devastating effect of the IRA bombing campaign, serious rioting in Derry in which two local men died and the persistence of 'no go' areas in nationalist parts of Derry and Belfast caused unionist pressure for more severe security measures. These proved irresistible. Fatefully, Faulkner advocated internment; it had been successfully implemented during the 1956-1962 campaign, when he had been Minister of Home Affairs. He hoped that it might now be equally effective without at the same time increasing his dependence on Britain. The Conservative leadership gave approval and at dawn, on 9 August 1971, over 330 suspects were 'lifted'. Violence immediately flared in Derry and Belfast and, by 11 August, 7,000 'refugees' were said to have fled south.

British ministers had shared the belief that internment might have a favourable impact. They were also deeply anxious to shore up Faulkner's position. If his government collapsed, there was no prospect of any local politician being any more successful and they would therefore have no alternative but to impose direct rule, an action which in itself was unlikely to improve the situation. Moreover, even within Wilson's Labour government, the marginal impact of its reform programme had been deeply disillusioning and ministers had gradually placed more stress on an aggressive stance against the IRA. Under Heath (Prime Minister from 19 June 1970), liberal legislation was increasingly postponed on the implicit assumption that it could only be introduced successfully when order had been restored to the streets. In effect, the British army became the main instrument of policy. Troop numbers rose by 6,000 between 1969 and 1972, and their powers were increased to make arrests, search property and operate checkpoints.

Internment was a disastrously mistaken policy. In part, this was because security force intelligence was simply inadequate. As a result, of the 1,260 in total arrested, 625 were released. Allegations that internees were mistreated in an effort to extract incriminating evidence was later corroborated in fourteen cases by an official government report. The interrogation techniques used were later described as 'inhuman and degrading' by the European Court at Strasbourg. This along with prisoner hunger strikes, heightened the negative effect of the mass arrests. The security forces, moreover, failed to entrap the young hard-core republican activists. Instead, many older IRA men were 'lifted'; many of these had hitherto opposed the Provisionals' violence but now came to support it wholeheartedly. PIRA recruitment and, in consequence, the number of bombings and shootings rose dramatically; of 173 deaths from political violence in 1971, 143 occurred after 9 August.

Nor were the likely political consequences of internment adequately considered. It alienated moderate Catholic opinion, both middle and working class. Recruitment from the nationalist minority to the UDR halved. (Initially, in 1970, its membership was 20 percent Catholic; by late 1971, 8 percent.) NICRA began a campaign of civil disobedience. To retain credibility within its own community, the SDLP withdrew from public life and withheld all co-operation from the government. Five MPs began a forty-eight hour hunger strike outside 10 Downing Street whilst the party leadership instigated a rent and rates strike, soon supported by *circa* 16,000 council house tenants. Along with the Dublin government and the Catholic church, it also condemned the upsurge in violence but in such measured terms that unionists interpreted their statements as coded approval. The collapse of any backing, even from constitutional nationalists, signalled the likely end both of Faulkner's administration and of Stormont itself. David Bleakley, the only non-unionist cabinet member, resigned. So also did William Craig, the hard-line Minister of Home Affairs. He did so in order to mobilise resistance to direct rule which now seemed imminent; (in April, Harold Wilson had said that a bill for this purpose had existed.) He formed the Vanguard Party, which had close contacts with the UVF.

No Cross-Border Intervention

In Britain, the operation of internment prompted strong Labour criticism of Heath's government. Wilson proposed, in the short term, the formation of a joint commission to monitor Stormont and suggested that within fifteen years Ireland be united within the Commonwealth. In Dublin, Jack Lynch was at no point consulted regarding the introduction of internment, even though past experience indicated that his government would have been required to implement it simultaneously if it was to have any hope of success; a number of leading republicans fled south as soon as it was applied. Lynch's cabinet had been considering its introduction in late 1970 but opinion steadily moved against, partly because Heath's government was coming to rely so heavily on a military response to the northern 'Troubles'. The Taoiseach denounced the mass arrests, set up an enquiry into security force brutality in the Six Counties and called for a UN observer to be dispatched there, as well as Stormont's abolition. As the violence rose subsequently, emergency measures had to be taken by the Dáil. In late 1972 Sinn Féin headquarters in Dublin's Kevin Street were closed, prominent IRA figures arrested and a special, no-jury, criminal court established.

However, throughout, Lynch (and his successors) preserved a policy of no direct intervention across the border. He lacked the military capacity and the will to intervene and force radical change and feared that the violence would spread south and threaten the stability of Ireland's democratic institutions. Moreover, he was advised against precipitate action by most responsible northern nationalist leaders. Though he favoured unity and saw Britain as an obstacle to it, he accepted that there should be no change in Northern Ireland's constitutional status without the consent of the majority there. Meanwhile, strongly influenced by the SDLP, he supported constitutional change to accommodate both traditions and sought to act as minority guarantor in tri-partite contacts with Westminster and Stormont.

Faced with the virtual collapse of order (fifteen died in a UVF bomb at McGurk's Bar in nationalist north Belfast, 4 December 1971) and diametrically conflicting pressures (for more radical reform and to repeal all recent liberal measures), Faulkner strove to strengthen his government. He appointed a Catholic to his cabinet, G B Newe. He also produced reports to highlight how many of the original civil rights had been met: in essence all but the repeal of the Special Powers Act. In addition, he indicated his support for further constitutional change. He favoured the use of proportional representation in local parliamentary elections but opposed 'power-sharing' with the nationalist parties as they did not support the Union and he claimed it would not affect the level of violence.

'Bloody Sunday'

'Bloody Sunday' proved to be the breaking point for the Stormont regime. A civil rights march was organised in Derry for 30 January 1972, in defiance of the ban imposed on all processions in July 1970. Faulkner's government interpreted the proposed demonstration as a direct challenge to its authority. Nonetheless, the strategy adopted by the 1st Parachute Regiment, which was given responsibility for policing it, was intended to be generally low-key – to confine the marchers to the Bogside, still a 'no go' area, but to deal resolutely with any hooligans or snipers. The troops lacked training in riot control and, once more, adequate intelligence. As the event proceeded, they came to believe that they were being fired on (some of the participants were armed with pistols but none of the soldiers was injured). They fired 108 rounds, causing the deaths of thirteen men, none of whom was proven to have been handling a firearm or a bomb at the time. A later government enquiry (under Lord Widgery) concluded that the Parachute Regiment's response 'bordered on the reckless' but found that it had been fired on first and that the illegal march had in itself created 'a highly dangerous situation'. No public enquiry was ever held but the city's coroner reached a very different verdict, describing the military action as 'unadulterated murder'. Civil rights leaders condemned it as 'another Sharpeville'; in the Commons, Bernadette Devlin, MP, struck the British Home Secretary, Reginald Maudling. Jack Lynch considered that it had been an 'unwarranted attack on unarmed civilians' and called for an international enquiry into the British army's role in the province.

CHAPTER 10

The Fall of Stormont

Many nationalists throughout Ireland considered that 'Bloody Sunday' had given the PIRA a mandate for its campaign. In Dublin, the burning down of the British Embassy (on 2 February) indicated the strength of popular feeling. At Westminster, the events in Derry reinforced the view that Stormont had now become a liability. Under strong pressure from abroad and from the Labour opposition to act decisively, Heath demanded, on 22 March, that Faulkner hand over total control of security to London. Faulkner refused and resigned next day. On 24 March 1972, direct rule was imposed on Northern Ireland and the regional government and parliament were suspended, initially for one year. A Secretary of State, William Whitelaw, took over the executive authority, previously exercised by the Stormont cabinet. Fifty years of unionist rule had ended.

In London, it was hoped that direct rule would bring calm to the province. The Stormont reform programme was continued but from the outset with little prospect of success, given the degree of nationalist distrust and the impossibility of satisfying both sides. British ministers promised an end to internment (almost 900 cases were eventually reviewed) and plebiscites on the border question, both of which demands Faulkner had accepted. They also indicated that the Special Powers Act would be examined and talks held with both local politicians and paramilitaries in an attempt to establish common ground and quickly restore devolved government.

PIRA Cease-Fire, Summer 1972

In mid-1972, the British government initiated negotiations with Sinn Féin in order to encourage political responses, explore its position given the new circumstances and at least create a breathing space in the violence. The republican leadership was responsive to Westminster's approach. PIRA had earlier issued 'peace terms', which included the abolition of Stormont, an end to British army violence and compensation for its victims and the release of prisoners. Throughout the years 1972-1975, Provisional confidence of quick victory abounded. Despite mass internment, its campaign had intensified and its popularity and military credibility had reached peak levels. In the short period of its existence, it had largely dictated the pattern of Westminster's policy towards the province. It could legitimately regard the collapse of Stormont as its most momentous achievement so far. It called a 'bi-lateral truce' which began on 26 June and Gerry Adams, released from prison for the purpose, led a delegation to attend secret talks with Whitelaw in London. Though the talks succeeded in winning 'special category status' (POW status) for republican prisoners and key PIRA activists were permitted to carry arms, Britain made no commitment to withdraw from Northern Ireland. On 9 July, amidst claims that the British army had broken the terms of the cease-fire, the physical force campaign resumed. Twelve days later, on 'Bloody Friday', 22 bombs exploded in Belfast, killing nine people.

The year 1972 proved to be by far the most violent of the current Northern Ireland 'Troubles' – 467 persons died and there were 10,600 shooting incidents and 1,380 explosions. A range of security measures was implemented. On 31 July, the army entered the 'no go' areas in Belfast and Derry during 'Operation Motorman'. The Special Powers Act was repealed. The operation of internment was modified as it had so antagonised nationalist opinion and had manifestly damaged Britain's reputation abroad. Moreover, it suggested that the violence was political rather than criminal as British ministers claimed. It was at first replaced (in 1972-1975) by a system of 'detention', under which suspects who were arrested were given increased legal rights (470 were detained, July 1973-October 1974). Later, in July 1973, new legislation, the Emergency Provisions Act, provided for arrest on suspicion and trial in certain scheduled political offences in so-called 'Diplock courts', where a single judge presided. It was an attempt to increase convictions by counteracting the intimidation of jurors and witnesses. In such cases, a heavy reliance was placed on the confessions of those charged. There were subsequently allegations of unfair interrogation methods being used by the RUC. These were corroborated by later official enquiry, which led to a significant modification of the techniques applied.

The Sunningdale Executive 1973-1974

At Westminster, security and reform measures alone were not thought to be sufficient response to the Northern Ireland question. During the early 1970s, a number of constitutional initiatives was attempted. Ministers were anxious to end direct rule from London; they were also responding to international and internal pressure to take decisive steps to resolve the conflict and had genuine hopes that a devolved government in Belfast could restore political stability and facilitate economic revival. Each scheme proposed had some element of 'power-sharing' between Unionists and nationalists and some Irish government involvement (an 'Irish dimension'). These features were included in order to correct the presumed defects in the failed Stormont system. They indicated a recognition that Northern Ireland required different treatment from other regions of the United Kingdom and that conflicting national identity, British or Irish, was at the heart of the problem.

The Sunningdale Executive came closer to success than any previous initiative. After talks with local politicians, the Conservative government produced broad proposals in March 1973 for the formation of an Assembly in Northern Ireland. It was to have limited legislative and executive powers (these did not include law and order) and there was also provision for 'power-sharing' and a vague 'Irish dimension'. In June, voting under proportional representation took place and in November some leading Unionist and nationalist politicians agreed to form a power-sharing executive under Faulkner's leadership. It was the first, and indeed the only, cross-community cabinet ever formed in Northern Ireland's history. Its members then proceeded to hammer out the details of the scheme during talks with British and Irish ministers at Sunningdale. These included the creation of a Council of Ireland and of a North/South commission to co-ordinate security. On 1 January 1974, the new government took office.

The Executive's greatest achievement lay in its formation rather than in its performance. Over the next five months it completed no legislation, its various committees proved ineffective and the Assembly itself frequently dissolved into chaos. Though cabinet members agreed on aims, they suffered throughout from acute internal strains, even within their narrowly circumscribed powers. The speed of the Executive's collapse was mainly due to lack of popular support. Already in the elections to the Assembly, anti-Sunningdale parties attracted 35 percent of the vote; by the time of the Westminster elections in February 1974 this had risen to 51 percent. The upward trend was due in part to the widespread perception amongst unionists that the Republic was failing to co-operate adequately in security matters (e.g. the extradition of republican suspects) and also their irritation at its unwillingness to amend Articles 2 and 3 of its Constitution. They were not reassured by the existence of a Fine Gael-dominated coalition government in Dublin (1973-1977) some of whose members regarded the southern claim to the North as Irish imperialism. (In 1976, it proceeded to ban all media interviews with republican activists, ten years before similar legislation was introduced in Britain.) A number of outrages on 17 May 1974 provide an insight into the mood of militant loyalists. In Dublin, 22 people were killed by car bombs which exploded without warning and five died in similar circumstances in Monaghan town. Two of the three vehicles used in the capital had earlier been hijacked in Protestant areas of Belfast.

In addition, many unionists were uneasy about power-sharing with nationalists. Yet more viewed with suspicion nationalist enthusiasm for the Council of Ireland. The SDLP had insisted that the Executive should formally approve its powers, membership and structures before agreeing policies for Northern Ireland. This approach had prompted Westminster government criticism but the party's leaders regarded power-sharing as insufficient in itself to reassure the minority, especially given the continued operation of internment.

Furthermore, the process of RUC reform was in its view so incomplete that they could not fully endorse the force, even as ministers.

The Council of Ireland proposals were rejected by the Ulster Unionist Party, prompting Faulkner's resignation as leader and his formation of a new party. They also precipitated the Ulster Workers' Council strike which began on 14 May 1974. Loyalist paramilitaries, trade union leaders and some unionist politicians combined to mobilise the industrial strength of the Protestant working class in a bid to overthrow the Executive. Electricity was rapidly reduced to emergency levels, most industry was brought to a standstill, main roads were blocked and the ports virtually closed. Though the devastating impact of the strike was heightened by intimidation (Wilson denounced the 'thugs and bullies'), it was passively supported throughout by most unionists. Despite appeals by the SDLP, Labour ministers refused to confront the militants. They were anxious to avoid a war on two fronts in Northern Ireland; in any case, the troops could not operate the vital electricity generating plant at Ballylumford in County Antrim and it was evident by then that the Executive lacked sufficient electoral support. On 28 May, the government collapsed; Faulkner and other unionist ministers resigned after the SDLP and Westminster had rejected a proposal to open negotiations with the strike leaders.

The fall of the Sunningdale Executive is illuminating. Despite its failure, Westminster remained anxious to establish a devolved government in Belfast but continued to insist on power-sharing and some role for the Republic. It hoped for new and constructive constitutional proposals and an open, pragmatic approach from Ulster's politicians. But it found the unionist parties resistant, destructive and divided amongst themselves. For them, the fall of Stormont was a defining moment. At a stroke, it removed their major bulwark against Irish nationalism and unity and also cut them off from civil service advisors, so seriously impairing the quality of their ideas. In addition, their leaders' powers of patronage shrank, so accentuating their disunity. Thereafter, they felt themselves to be, and indeed were, more isolated, vulnerable and impotent. They were therefore suspicious of any new initiatives, fearing that these would advance nationalist objectives, that the North's UK status would be compromised and that Britain would 'sell them out'. They became, justifiably, associated in the media with negativism and a refusal to participate in imaginative dialogue. Many observers had, from the outset, little sympathy for a movement which they identified with ancient privilege and recent sectarian oppression.

Paisley's DUP embodied an irrationality and an aggressive narrow defence of Protestant interests. Its leadership, flushed by the success of the UWC strike, arrogantly concluded that it could and should now determine the form of any devolved structures in Ulster. It pressed for a return to majority rule and Stormont's restitution. More moderate unionists acknowledged that this was unobtainable and therefore became reconciled to direct rule. It at least preserved the Union intact and might, in time, reduce the violence to an 'acceptable level'. In contrast, the SDLP was productive of ideas and seemed progressive and positive in its approach. To unionist dismay, it was warmly received, and enjoyed influence, amongst ministers and officials, not only in Dublin but in London. The fact that it could hold out the prospect of peace, if the causes of nationalist alienation were resolved, heightened its political leverage. Its anti-imperialist/nationalist interpretation of

Ulster politics was accepted by the British Labour Party as well as in southern Ireland, amongst Irish-Americans and within the European Community. The minority's experience of 'fifty years of unionist misrule' guaranteed its representatives much international media sympathy. Its leaders also benefited globally from any residual anti-British sentiment.

Further Attempts at Devolution

Though the level of violence in Ulster dropped from its 1972 peak, it still so polarised and embittered opinion there that prospects for an agreed political solution based on inter-communal compromise steadily receded. Britain's persistent attempts at devolution were therefore intended in part to satisfy world opinion that every effort was being made to solve a clearly intractable problem. In 1975, Merlyn Rees, Labour Secretary of State, organised a Constitutional Convention. Government ministers indicated that if it could produce a settlement which attracted broad inter-communal support this would be implemented by Westminster. They merely provided it with loose guidelines: Sunningdale's failure was attributed largely to Dublin and London imposing their own terms too much on local politicians. The initiative proved to be a predictable failure. In the May 1975 election, the hard-line United Ulster Unionist Council, which favoured the restoration of Stormont, won 55 percent of the votes cast whilst parties favouring power-sharing attracted under 43 percent. The resulting draft report in November therefore proposed a return to majority (unionist) rule as in the 1920 Act and made no provision for an Irish dimension. This was as unacceptable to Westminster as it was to the SDLP.

Another PIRA Cease-Fire

There was some contemporary speculation that Britain might withdraw from Northern Ireland, based on earlier statements by Wilson and pre-Convention hints to this effect by Labour ministers. No doubt these reflected a genuine weariness with the problem. Possibly they were also made to pressurise the unionist parties into adopting more moderate negotiating positions and also in the hope of drawing the PIRA into further negotiations; 100 bombs had exploded in Britain during 1973-74, killing 47 people (over half of these had died and 230 had been injured in no-warning explosions at pubs in Guildford, Surrey and Birmingham).

Against the background of a low level of security in Ulster, secret government overtures were made, and a cease-fire eventually brokered, beginning on 22 December 1974. A group of Protestant clergy had acted as intermediaries, meeting Provisional leaders at Feakle, in County Clare, two weeks earlier. British ministers agreed to finance Sinn Féin-manned 'incident centres' in nationalist areas, to monitor its operation and defuse volatile situations. They proceeded to offer generous terms. These included a guaranteed place for PIRA at any future negotiating table, the release of republican internees and transfer of those held in Britain to Northern Ireland and British troop withdrawal if the peace held. Rees had appealed for 'a genuine and sustained cessation of violence'. However, within six weeks, when it seemed clear that Irish unity was not on offer, the campaign resumed. The cease-fire had, in any case, never been complete. Some volunteers had ignored it throughout its duration, tit-for-tat murders had occurred between republicans and the UVF in Belfast and south Armagh and a violent feud simmered between

Provisional units and Official IRA members. Overall, it damaged the organisational cohesion and collective morale of PIRA. In 1975, its members were exclusively conducting an 'armed struggle' – without it there was no campaign at all.

New Security Initiatives

Thereafter, Westminster politicians from both major parties came to accept that there would be no quick, radical breakthrough in Northern Ireland. Rees's successor, Roy Mason, held his own talks with local parties about devolution but due to lack of consensus and enthusiasm, took no further action. Otherwise he was hawkish, defending direct rule, down-playing any Irish dimension to the conflict and concentrating mainly on restoring order. The broad direction of security policy towards 'criminalisation' was accelerated. This meant the adoption, as far as possible, of ordinary legal procedures in response to the province's violence, in part to encourage the perception that its roots were, as ministers claimed, criminal rather than political. (A Defence Ministry ruling in November 1974 stated that names of soldiers killed in Northern Ireland should not be added to war memorials as the area was not classed as a war zone.) Thus the detention of republican suspects was phased out by December 1975, and during the following year PIRA prisoners were deprived of the special category (i.e. POW) status granted them in 1972.

Meanwhile after the Birmingham pub bombings in November 1974, the Prevention of Terrorism Act was passed. This proscribed the IRA in Britain and increased police powers to arrest and detain persons arriving from Northern Ireland or to exclude them altogether; this was done in part to prevent an anti-Irish backlash. For political reasons, the Labour government also sought to encourage the 'Ulsterisation' of the conflict. This was intended to reinforce the view that it was an internal UK problem and amenable to normal policing methods. Thus the number and role of British troops in the Six Counties, were both reduced (troop numbers fell by 6,000 between 1972 and 1976) and the local policing services – the RUC, police reserve, and UDR – were expanded to compensate. In the republican heartland of south Armagh, however, the Special Air Service (SAS) had to be deployed from January 1976 so exposing the limits to this policy of 'police primacy'.

Economic and Social Measures

Westminster's response to the Northern Ireland problem was at no time confined to security measures and devolution schemes. Simultaneously, steps were taken to assist distressed local firms and to stimulate the Ulster economy in the hope of reducing the level of violence and counter-acting its disastrous negative impact on investment. These included labour training schemes, agencies formed to advise and assist commercial enterprise and a range of grants to help it meet its capital requirements.

By 1981, 45 percent of industrial workers in the North were working for manufacturers receiving financial aid from the government. John De Lorean's car construction company was the most risky venture to be given support. An American businessman, he was offered £77 million of public funds to begin production in west Belfast. In 1978 he promised to employ 2,600 workers within five years; by 1982 his factory had collapsed in bankruptcy with the loss of 1,500 jobs. His most enduring legacy was in celluloid – the futuristic gull-winged vehicle used for time travel in the *Back to the Future* films.

To help legitimise the State within the minority community, Westminster also introduced measures to eliminate sectarian discrimination in employment. Government bodies were established for this purpose, relevant research encouraged and improved means of redress provided for individuals. Generally, these initiatives suffered from inadequate legal powers and insufficient funding. Parallel steps were taken to ensure the fair allocation of public housing. In addition, by 1981 government expenditure on house construction in Northern Ireland per head of population was four times higher than in England and Wales.

Overall, the broad impact of Labour's policies from 1974 to 1979 was to antagonise, rather than reassure, northern nationalists. They were dismayed by the emphasis on 'Ulsterisation' and 'criminalisation' regarding security, by the evidence from current government enquiries of dubious interrogation techniques having been practised by the RUC and by the absence of any substantive role for the southern Irish government in Rees's 1975 Convention proposal. Their irritation rose further when James Callaghan decided to increase by five the number of Ulster MPs at Westminster, so, it seemed, strengthening direct rule from London. This contributed directly to his government's fall. When it lost a vital Commons division, 311 votes to 310, on 28 March 1979, the two northern nationalist members in the House, Gerry Fitt, SDLP leader and Frank Maguire, had both abstained.

PIRA Prepare for a 'Long War'

After 1975, PIRA likewise reappraised its strategy. Leading Ulster activists, Gerry Adams and Brian Keenan in particular, also recognised that there would be no quick victory but rather a 'long war'. They successfully urged on the movement the necessity for a 'twin-track' approach. On the military side, significant organisational refinements were adopted, based on their proposals and in response to recent British security measures. The training of volunteers in interrogation techniques was improved. More importantly, a secretive PIRA structure was devised; open battalions and companies were replaced by underground cells, despite the implicit risk that this might cause an unhelpful isolation from its own communities. At the same time, however, it was decided to expand the movement's political involvement. Its virtual non-existence had been exposed during the 1974/75 cease-fire and had prompted much northern criticism of the Dublin leadership at the time. Consequently, a number of the incident centres opened then were retained as a means of increasing republican control of minority areas. Also, under IRA direction, Sinn Féin appointed full-time organisers to improve publicity, agitate on popular issues, infiltrate local organisations and generally broaden and expand support.

The H-Block Hunger Strike

These structural and tactical changes proved to be only a limited success. In 1976, a peace movement (the 'Peace People') emerged amongst women in west Belfast. Its founders, Betty Williams and Mairead Corrigan, were later awarded the Nobel Peace Prize. It provided clear evidence of growing war weariness. These sentiments were strengthened when Pope John Paul II appealed for peace 'on bended knee' at Drogheda in September 1979. At the same time, special category status for IRA prisoners was being phased out as part of the government's 'criminalisation' strategy. The prisoners resisted the changes (the loss of free association and of the right to wear their own clothes, etc), by going 'on the blanket' (i.e. refusing to wear prison uniform) and on the 'dirty protest' (i.e. smearing their cells with excrement rather than slopping out). Cardinal Ó Fiaich, Ireland's Catholic Primate, described their conditions as 'inhuman'. By 1979, however, their protest campaign was crumbling, with individuals opting out rather than forfeiting their claims to remission. Bobby Sands, Officer Commanding in the Maze Prison, observed that they had 'failed to engage any active support, outside our immediate hard core' – i.e. republican militants, relatives and friends. They needed, in his view, to 'broaden the battlefield'. He was convinced that the special category issue could be used to mobilise mass support and that human sacrifice by the prisoners themselves could puncture popular indifference. By late 1980, the first Provisional hunger strike had ignominiously collapsed after six weeks. On 1 March 1981, however, Sands himself led a second. From the outset, it was clear that he and others were prepared to die unless their demands were met.

The political impact of the prisoners' action was traumatic. Outside, sympathetic pressure groups formed, comprised not just of relatives but of politicians, trade unionists and students. The Maze H-blocks almost instantly became the focus of massive media attention. Visitors to the prison included a papal envoy, and representatives of the southern government, which meanwhile raised the issue with the US president. A new political opportunity arose with the death of Frank Maguire. He had been, since 1974, the independent Nationalist MP at Westminster for Fermanagh/South Tyrone, with a 5,000 majority and was himself an ex-IRA internee. Sinn Féin nominated Sands as candidate in the resulting by-election. Due to moral blackmail and intimidation he was unopposed by the SDLP or any other nationalist representative. His victory was the first sign of the 'broad anti-imperialist front' which Adams, his campaign manager, ultimately aimed for. One of his campaign slogans was: 'His life can be saved if you vote for him'. His victory by 1,450 votes was the main watershed in PIRA history after Stormont fell. It provided stark evidence that the Provisionals' campaign had significant electoral backing. On 5 May 1981, after 66 days of fasting, Sands died, having solidified support for the prisoners and their cause and dramatically magnified political tensions throughout the North.

Several weeks later, at short notice, Sinn Féin sought to take advantage of the 11 June 1981 General Election in the Republic; nine H-Block prisoners stood. This contest provided an opportunity for the party to test its electoral strength in the twenty-six counties without raising the vexed question of the legitimacy of the southern parliament; none of its candidates could, after all, take their seats. (For them to have given the Dáil such recognition would have split the movement from top to bottom.) The outcome was highly satisfactory; two of them were successful. This represented a vital loss for Fianna Fáil in a close contest and resulted in a Fine Gael/Labour coalition returning briefly to office under Garrett FitzGerald. He immediately sought to act as intermediary in the prison disputes.

Meanwhile, the prisoners' death toll continued to

rise, finally reaching ten. However, its political impact was diminishing and the hunger strike itself was losing momentum. The PIRA leadership found compromise, especially after such sacrifice, difficult. The deadlock was broken when the families of those refusing food indicated that they would seek medical help once their relatives became unconscious. A local priest, Father Denis Faul, led them in a delegation to the Northern Ireland Office in early October and they agreed terms, the essentials of which had been on offer since June. Without this intervention, the strike might well have continued until inevitable and chaotic collapse, resulting in minority revulsion as deaths mounted, PIRA isolation and the loss of Sinn Féin's electoral gains.

CHAPTER 11

The Ballot Box and the Armalite

As it was, northern urban activists (Gerry Adams, etc) within Sinn Féin and the IRA, proceeded to exploit the political gains of the strike and, in the process, succeeded in asserting their own overall leadership of the movement. The experience of the H-Block agitation had reinforced their view that the 'ballot bomb' (i.e. politics) could be a valuable adjunct to the physical force campaign. This opinion was graphically expressed by ex-internee Danny Morrison – media spokesperson for the fasting prisoners during the hunger strike – at the Sinn Féin Árd Fheis. He stated: 'Will anyone here object if, with the ballot paper in this hand and an Armalite in this hand, we take power in Ireland?' But he urged: 'Political activity won't get the Brits out, the IRA will.' Soon afterwards, Adams made a further electoral breakthrough for Sinn Féin by winning West Belfast (June 1983) and was elected Party President, displacing Ruairí Ó Brádaigh in November 1983.

Eventually, in 1986, the Sinn Féin party formally abandoned its policy of abstention from the southern Dáil, an issue which it had been able to avoid in 1981. Predictably, as a result, the movement was split; the old Dublin leadership withdrew in protest, regarding the decision as a betrayal of their ideal – a thirty-two county republic. They immediately formed Republican Sinn Féin. Belatedly, in that same year, the PIRA held a general army convention, its first since 1970, at which it ratified Sinn Féin's increased political involvement. But it did so on condition that its physical force campaign should in no way be compromised. Had these terms proved unacceptable, further division within the republican movement would have been unavoidable. At the time, vital preparations were in hand for an intensification of Provisional activities. These included a recruitment drive in Éire in order to escalate bombing operations in England and highly-productive negotiations with the Libyan authorities regarding possible arms shipments. The Armalite/ballot box strategy proved in the end to be only partially successful; nonetheless it was the most formative influence on northern politics throughout the 1980s.

The Loyalist Paramilitaries

By comparison, the loyalist paramilitaries were infinitely less resourceful or pragmatic than the Provisionals; they did, however, operate in a much less favourable context. The UWC strike in 1974 proved to be their high point. Their subsequent assumption that they would play a credible and significant political role proved totally misplaced. Thereafter, they were 'frozen out' by respectable unionist politicians. At the same time, their level of support dropped sharply; their brand of pro-State terror was increasingly regarded as irrelevant and unnecessary by their own communities during the late 1970s and early 1980s when the security forces became more effective in combating the PIRA. They were unable to compete against the traditional political parties or established agencies of the State – police, army, courts – all of which survived despite the context of instability. These circumstances accentuated their difficulties in attracting competent recruits. The Protestant middle class rarely at any time treated them with other than disdain, whilst able and patriotic members of the working-class, who wished to serve queen and country, increasingly joined the RUC and UDR rather than the UVF or UDA. In contrast, the IRA was able to exploit the broad alienation of the minority as a whole from the State – its reluctance to use government agencies (e.g. the police) its scepticism about state propaganda and culture and its consequent responsiveness to community action (e.g. the promotion of the Irish language). The Provisionals have been able, therefore, consistently to attract recruits from a wider range of social backgrounds. They have particularly benefited from university-educated, potentially middle-class involvement. This has helped them to hone their military campaign and also to develop their ideas, present their case and so expand their appeal.

The loyalist paramilitaries have generally not had any political wing equivalent to Sinn Féin to justify and explain their actions. They have produced very few articulate spokesmen and have had great difficulty in developing a distinct political agenda. The UVF's forages into politics have been brief, erratic and narrowly-focused. They have amounted to little more than the occasional pressure group, voicing opposition to no-jury trials, supporting internee release and seeking to improve prison conditions. The issues it raised have no appeal within the broader unionist electorate. By and large, its members have resigned themselves to not being a significant force in local politics. They joined the force from a blend of patriotism, sectarianism and thuggery. Most considered that their best way to defend the State was through direct action, mainly sectarian murder.

The UDA with its initially larger and more respectable membership has periodically attempted to seize the political initiative. In the mid-1970s, a minority grouping within it argued forcefully for negotiated independence as the only possible 'common denominator' for Ulstermen, a possible 'third way'. Some British politicians encouraged this 'Ulster nationalism' (Rees), hoping that it might be used to distance the province from Britain and also to encourage its promulgators into active politics. But for unionists generally it has always been the least appealing option as it would destroy the Union, and so play into nationalist hands and would likely exacerbate the difficulties of the regional economy. The electoral value of this proposal was therefore negligible.

Elements within the UDA have also promoted a revised version of Ulster's history to counteract the republican slogan of 'Brits out'. This claimed that the medieval Gaels displaced the indigenous Pictish Cruithen, who withdrew to Scotland but then returned centuries later to resettle their original homelands during the sixteenth and seventeenth century plantations. This implies that the Protestant Ulster Scots (the Cruithin) and not the Celtic invaders (Catholic Gaels) were the first occupants of the north-east and therefore not recently arrived 'Brits' or 'planters'. Once again, these ideas have generated little interest within either the movement's rank and file or the Protestant community at large.

Overall, the loyalists' inability to develop a distinct political position, their record of vicious sectarian killing and their reputation for incompetence have consistently alienated Protestant sympathy. (In February 1979, eleven Protestants, known as the 'Shankill Butchers', each received life imprisonment for offences which included nineteen murders). Their resulting lack of funds which, unlike the IRA, is not compensated for by backing from abroad, has caused a dependence on extortion and theft further damaging recruitment, morale and support. Even in staunchly unionist areas, their members have rarely attracted more than two to three percent of the votes in any form of election. The fact that the government has acted far more effectively against pro-State than republican terrorists, provides the most eloquent evidence of the shallowness of their support. Though republicans urge that loyalist collusion with the security forces is endemic, substantiated cases have been rare. Between 1980 and 1987, similar numbers of IRA and loyalist paramilitary members were charged with murder though the Provisionals had caused 386 deaths and the loyalists 69. During each of these years, the number of loyalists charged was generally greater than the number of their victims; for the IRA it was usually less than half.

Thatcher's Approach to Ulster

Initially, the Conservative government formed on 3 May 1979 placed much emphasis on security, as Labour had done toward the end of its administration. Under Margaret Thatcher the emergency legislation introduced in the 1970s was marginally amended and seemed to be assuming permanency. Despite the political tensions associated with the hunger strikes, the shift towards 'police primacy' continued. Some additional measures were, however, taken to combat terrorist activity in Europe. Also, due to adverse court decisions and damaging publicity, local police interrogation techniques had to be modified making convictions more difficult to obtain. Westminster's response to this problem was highly controversial, in particular its use of 'supergrasses', twenty-five in total between 1981 and 1983. These were known paramilitary members who had turned informer; most were given immunity from prosecution even though a number were murder suspects. Solely on the basis of their evidence, 600 persons were arrested and many later charged in no-jury Diplock courts. This process inevitably prompted criticism on the grounds of morality, reliability and cost. There was also much unease at mounting, though inconclusive, evidence from the late 1970s of a 'shoot to kill' policy being adopted by the security forces, even in circumstances where they were under no direct physical threat.

Like its predecessors, the new Conservative government by no means relied exclusively on security in its response to the Northern Ireland question. It too introduced a variety of economic, social and constitutional measures, and also treated Northern Ireland as a special case. Its policies were much less ideologically driven when applied to the North than elsewhere in Great Britain; the 'Thatcher revolution' was diluted when it crossed the Irish Sea. Though there were moves towards the privatisation of state-owned firms and the owner-occupancy of homes rose, public grants to local private enterprise and spending on housing remained high relative to other parts of the United Kingdom. In addition, a new agency, the Fair Employment Commission, was set up in 1986, partly as a result of US pressure. It had increased funding and more powers than its forerunner (the Fair Employment Agency) but it had the same purpose – to eliminate religious discrimination in employment. These wide-ranging approaches had a limited impact. Unemployment rose throughout the early 1980s, regional growth rates were consistently lower than in Great Britain and adult male unemployment amongst Catholics remained two and a half times higher than amongst Protestants.

Further Failed Attempts at Devolution

The constitutional initiatives taken by the Conservatives proved to be by far the most original and least expected aspects of their policy. The party's manifesto in 1979 contained a commitment merely to increase council powers in the province, successive attempts at devolution under Labour having failed. But this was not implemented. The Irish National Liberation Army (INLA) assassination in March 1979 of Airey Neave (shadow Northern Ireland Secretary) by a bomb in his car at Westminster removed its main enthusiast. (This illegal republican paramilitary group had appeared in 1975, drawing some of its members from the IRA volunteers who opposed the cease-fires of 1972 and 1975. It rapidly acquired a reputation for ruthlessness). There was also powerful nationalist opposition to the proposal.

Instead, two further attempts were made at setting up a regional government in Belfast. British ministers were under strong pressure from Labour, Dublin and the United States to act decisively to restore stability, amidst the passions generated by the Maze hunger strikes. More in hope than expectation, therefore, a conference of local politicians was called in early 1980 by Humphrey Atkins, Northern Ireland's Secretary, to discuss devolution. It collapsed quickly without agreement. In September his successor, James Prior, tried a different approach, 'rolling devolution'. This provided for the election of an assembly in the Six Counties, initially to supervise the activities of the Northern Ireland Office but empowered to take over some of its functions if members could reach cross-party agreement. Legislation was passed and elections held but again no progress was made. Abstention by the SDLP eliminated any prospect of cross-sectional consensus.

Both initiatives highlighted the irreconcilibility of the respective party positions. The DUP favoured devolution. It demanded a modified Stormont with majority rule, no built-in power-sharing and no Irish dimension. The Unionist Party regarded the basic thrust of Britain's devolutionary proposals as a threat to the Union and its leaders, therefore, favoured continued direct rule from London to consolidate Northern Ireland's place within the Union. They would have welcomed local government reform. The SDLP had been wary of both recent initiatives, largely because of the vague nature of any southern Irish dimension in each. John Hume, party leader from November 1979, having steadily become less interested in any internal northern settlement with an elected assembly which would inevitably be unionist-controlled, favoured an all-Ireland approach. He was also deeply concerned at Sinn Féin's new political strategy and early electoral success. In May 1983, along with the leaders of the main southern parties, he helped organise the New Ireland Forum in Dublin in order to encourage moderate nationalists and offer a constitutional alternative to Sinn Féin and the IRA. Its purpose was to reach an agreed approach to the northern question. There, Hume expressed his conviction that unity was the only solution. After 41 sessions and 317 submissions, the Forum produced a report in May 1984 which essentially reiterated this conclusion and backed a unitary Irish state as its option of first preference. Both a federal arrangement and joint London/Dublin authority in Northern Ireland were also thought worthy of consideration. The unionist parties, all of whom had refused to participate, regarded these findings as a typically unrealistic expression of old-style nationalism. British ministers described them as 'one-sided and unacceptable'. Thatcher, above all, dismayed southern leaders by dismissing their three proposed solutions with the phrase: 'Out, out, out.'

The Anglo-Irish Agreement

In these circumstances, the Conservatives' third initiative, the Anglo-Irish Agreement, signed by Thatcher and FitzGerald on 15 November 1985, came as an immense shock to unionists. It was the most ambitious attempt at an Irish settlement since the 1920s. It established a joint ministerial conference of British and Irish ministers, backed by a permanent secretariat at Maryfield, near Stormont. Its function was to meet regularly to discuss political, security and legal matters relating to the North; like Sunningdale, the Agreement illustrated to nationalists throughout Ireland that it was possible for the constitutional status of the Six Counties to be changed. For the first time, Dublin's right to be consulted on its internal administration was both recognised and formalised. In the process, the northern minority was offered, likewise for the first time, real recognition of its national identity and rights. Its leaders hoped that the bi-partisan approach of the two governments would eventually evolve into joint authority, even unity.

Unionists were not consulted about the Agreement and its institutions did not need either their consent or participation to operate. Article 1 was, however, included specifically for their reassurance. It stated that there would be no change in Northern Ireland's constitutional status without majority consent. Also, in the hope of moderating their negotiating position in the future, Dublin's consultative role was to be reduced if devolved power-sharing structures were successfully arrived at for the province. It was, of course, the case that this same clause provided the SDLP with an equally powerful disincentive to co-operate in establishing any agreed internal institutions. It clearly wished the Republic's role in the Six Counties to expand, and not diminish.

Overall, it was Britain that made the greater concessions. Éire's Constitution, after all, including Articles 2 and 3, remained unchanged and the Agreement was widely hailed in Dublin as a diplomatic triumph. In early 1985, few could have predicted that Mrs Thatcher would have agreed to such terms – she seemed sympathetic to the unionist perspective; by 1984, it was evident that Sinn Féin had peaked electorally and the level of violence in the North had dropped consistently through the early 1980s. Furthermore, Charles Haughey's emergence as leader of Fianna Fáil in December 1979 seemed to dim the prospects for such an accord. He made his party's position more hard-line, describing Northern Ireland as a 'failed entity', calling for Britain's withdrawal as the solution and demanding that the unionists accept unity. The Falklands' War was the prelude to the most bitter phase in Anglo-Irish relations in fifty years; when the Argentinians invaded the south Atlantic islands in April 1982 Thatcher retaliated immediately by despatching a taskforce. Its victory enabled her subsequently to overwhelm Labour's incipient recovery in the June 1983 Westminster elections. The Republic's defence minister, Patrick Power, described Britain as the aggressor in the dispute.

But powerful countervailing factors also existed. Like Hume, the Conservative leadership was concerned at Sinn Féin's electoral progress; if it continued, it would undermine Britain's traditional power-sharing approach to the North. At the same time Thatcher was under other powerful pressures – from Labour, the United States, the EEC and the UN – to seize the initiative in Ulster. There was a growing consensus in London and elsewhere that action was required. The region not only complicated Britain's international relations, it was also a significant financial drain, absorbed large numbers of troops and created acute security problems throughout the United Kingdom. (This was graphically illustrated by the bomb at the Grand Hotel, Brighton, HQ of the Conservative party conference, on 12 October 1984, when five died and Thatcher was among the thirty-four injured.) Yet, by the mid-1980s, none of the nation's vital strategic interests were at stake there.

The range of options open to Westminster was limited. Devolution attempts had repeatedly failed and British politicians had consistently resisted integration (i.e. making direct rule permanent). By instinct, Thatcher tended to favour a radical approach, and her massive majority, 144 in June 1983, provided her with ample opportunity. Her officials encouraged her to consider an Anglo-Irish initiative. Both she and they became convinced, partly on Hume's advice, that it would lead to substantial improvements in cross-border security co-operation. They mistakenly assumed that this, and an associated economic revival in the North would dampen Unionist opposition. In any case, Thatcher believed that the terms of the agreement she was considering would not weaken the Union, as Britain's legal sovereignty would be preserved intact.

Prospects for such an accord were enhanced when Garrett FitzGerald became Taoiseach. Even under Haughey, however, Anglo-Irish relations had progressed. He was pragmatic in office, in part because of his small majority, and set a pattern for southern leaders of negotiating with Britain over unionist heads. Mrs Thatcher was responsive. In 1980, the two premiers had agreed to meet regularly, made plans to discuss the 'totality of relations on these islands' and commissioned joint studies by officials of possible areas of North-South co-operation. FitzGerald's succession accelerated this process. He was liberal; he launched a 'Constitutional Crusade' to make the South a 'genuine republic', less 'sectarian' and thus more likely to 'appeal to unionists'. As part of this process he organised referenda on divorce and abortion and argued the case for a new Constitution. He regarded internal reconciliation in the North as a greater priority than unity. Under his governments, ministerial contacts with Britain increased; secret talks were held in 1983 and a series of discussions in 1985 culminated in the Agreement.

CHAPTER 12

The Agreement in Operation

By 1989, the joint ministerial conference resulting from the Agreement had met thirty times with its meetings becoming progressively more systematic and wide-ranging. The new bi-partisan approach suited both governments. Each expressed support for broadly similar objectives in the North, at least in the short term; these included devolution, the equal and fair recognition of both traditions and the adoption of fair employment practices. Éire's now formal consultative role in Ulster's administration reduced international criticism of Britain's policy there whilst all southern parties came to value the Republic's new status. Haughey alone had at first denounced the accord. He claimed that it made too many concessions to unionists and that it conflicted with the Forum Report and the Irish Constitution because it acknowledged British sovereignty over the Six Counties. Such was his hostility that it contributed to splits within Fianna Fáil and the formation of the Progressive Democrats by party dissidents in December 1985. Each was a factor in Haughey's failure to win an outright Dáil majority. When back in office in 1987, however, he had no option but to endorse publicly the Agreement, given its popularity in the South.

But the Conservative government's expectations that the structures created in 1985 would help contain and resolve the Ulster conflict proved to be entirely misplaced. Sinn Féin denounced them as a mechanism for tightening security, reinforcing partition and insulating Westminster from international criticism. The IRA intensified its campaign in an attempt to drive Britain beyond the Agreement's terms. It was well-equipped to do so. It imported an estimated 30 tons of arms between October 1985 and July 1986 and, in October 1986, 105 tons were landed at Wicklow from Libya to be moved North as required. Twelve months later, a further consignment of 120 tons from the same source was intercepted by the Irish authorities. (Anti-British sentiment had peaked in Libya after the UK had provided bases for US jets when they bombed Libya in early 1986.) Meanwhile loyalist paramilitary recruitment and activity had also increased. Their members threatened to shoot those collaborating with the accord and they were involved in protest riots, in random attacks on Catholics and on the homes of police officers attempting to preserve order. (Seventy-nine Catholic and fifty RUC families were fire-bombed in their homes between 1 and 26 April 1986.) In November they were responsible for four bomb explosions in Dublin. Overall, the level of violence rose sharply against a background of steeply rising unemployment. Between 1985 and 1988, the number of deaths per year rose from 54 to 93, shooting incidents from 237 to 537 and explosions from 148 to 253. These figures relate to some of the most brutal incidents of the entire Troubles.

Security Policy causes Strains

The security gains which British ministers assumed would flow from greater Anglo-Irish co-operation did not materialise. Though the Republic signed an extradition agreement in December 1987, Britain's repeated inability to have its terms implemented by Dublin strained inter-governmental relations. In defending its response, the South claimed with justification that grave miscarriages of justice were occurring in Britain. Firstly, in March 1991, the 'Birmingham Six' were released after serving seventeen years. They had been given life sentences for pub bombings (November 1974) in the city; the Appeal Court, however, eventually judged that these convictions were 'no longer safe and satisfactory'. Meanwhile, in October 1989, the 'Guildford Four' had been freed. They had likewise been given life sentences for their alleged part in London pub bombings (also in 1974). Their confessions, afterwards retracted, were no longer thought to provide sufficient proof of culpability. Moreover, the Dublin authorities expressed concern at Westminster's apparent quashing of an internal police enquiry into 'shoot to kill' allegations against the security forces and at Britain's general 'obsession' with security. They urged the need for comprehensive police reform, for UDR disbandment and for an increase in the number of judges in Diplock courts from one to three in order to reduce the northern minority's acute sense of alienation. But Britain, concerned about their likely impact on police and troop morale and fearing a deeply hostile Unionist reaction, hesitated to take these steps.

In the context of escalating violence, Westminster retained, amended and extended its major emergency legislation. In addition, new measures were taken: a broadcasting ban was imposed on spokespersons for, and supporters of, paramilitaries; all electoral candidates had to declare their 'opposition to the use of violence for political ends'; courts were empowered to draw inferences from a suspect's silence in court; penalties were increased for incitement to hatred and rights of procession were curtailed. Internment was recommended by the RUC but rejected due to anticipated nationalist opposition, and the inevitable damage to Britain's image abroad.

'Ulster Says No'

If Thatcher was disappointed by the Agreement's failure to ease Britain's security problems, she was equally surprised by the virulence of the opposition to it from unionists. She came to feel that she had alienated them without winning sufficient compensatory gains. Several factors account for the intensity of their hostility. They condemned the accord as a 'conspiracy' (as it was negotiated secretly without their consent) and as a negation of democracy because it was at variance with the will of the northern majority. They were also convinced that it had resulted in unbalanced political structures in which they would have little influence. They noted that under its terms, if any future devolved government was established in Belfast, the SDLP, a minority party, would be guaranteed cabinet posts. Furthermore, in its inter-ministerial conference, they feared that Britain would not support the unionist position but would instead adopt a neutral stance, whereas the Republic would articulate the views and champion the rights of northern nationalists. Finally, unionists were outraged that its terms should provide Dublin with a formal, consultative role in the administration of the Six Counties without having to make any reciprocal change in Articles 2 and 3 of its own Constitution. These clauses, according to a later Irish Supreme Court decision, imposed a 'Constitutional imperative' on southern ministers to 're-unify the national territory' whatever the terms of their agreement with Britain in 1985. Overall, the Unionist leader, James Molyneaux, believed that 'ten years of patient endeavour had been wiped out' by the accord. He and Paisley fervently believed that it would ultimately lead to the end of the Union. Both had been out-manoeuvred by their political opponents, especially John Hume, and had gravely over-estimated the warmth of their relationship with Mrs Thatcher.

The protest campaign orchestrated by the unionist leaders caused considerable disruption during the months following the Agreement. They organised mass protest demonstrations, called a 'day of action' (i.e. a strike) on 3 March 1986, encouraged supporters to refuse the payment of rates over a five-month period and brought to a temporary standstill the work of councils under their control. They withdrew consent from the British government and boycotted talks with Conservative ministers for almost two years. All the unionist members of Prior's assembly resigned their seats in order to create by-elections which they then fought on the single issue of opposition to the Agreement. The Ulster Unionist Party ended its special relationship with the Tories which dated back to its foundation one hundred years earlier.

Nonetheless, the response by unionists to the Agreement was more muted than it had been to Sunningdale in 1974. This was partly because the accord was so designed as to be immune to their protests. It did not require either their recognition nor their co-operation to survive, though the intensity of their agitation did impede its evolution towards joint authority or even unity. Also, their leaders were constrained in their opposition by the fact that if their actions seemed likely to weaken the Union with Britain, (e.g. by threatening the use of force or calling for independence) they would cause division within the ranks of their own movement. Weeks after a low turn-out of their erstwhile supporters in the 1987 Westminster election, their total boycott of talks with British ministers was called off. A significant proportion of party members had by then come to regard a purely negative campaign aimed at destroying the Agreement ('Ulster says No' was its best-known slogan) as simply inadequate. Academics, journalists and other politicians likewise implored Molyneaux and Paisley to be more constructive ('to come out of the bunker'). Both had, however, so passionately denounced the Agreement that they could not easily now accept its structures and participate, as Britain had hoped, in power-sharing devolution, even if this would lessen Dublin's role. (This approach could have been pursued inside Prior's assembly, which was not dissolved until June 1986.) The broad strategy which they gradually adopted was to attempt cautiously to rebuild their relationship with Westminster whilst putting forward alternative proposals of their own to replace the accord. Their aim was to achieve a complete political recovery, with the province's status within the United Kingdom unambiguously reaffirmed and accepted both in London and in Dublin. The Unionist Party's preference was, as before, for continued direct rule from Westminster with possibly some devolution of administrative responsibilities to local politicians. The DUP still favoured the establishment of an elected assembly in Belfast with powers similar to Stormont before abolition. Both parties were split over power-sharing with nationalists but unitedly opposed any Irish dimension; their leaders therefore rejected Haughey's offer of talks.

Arguably, the loyalist paramilitaries were more constructive and conciliatory in their approach. Frustrated by the apparent impotence of the major unionist parties and concerned by the alarming rise in violence after 1985, elements within the UDA attempted to seize the initiative. They produced a policy document, entitled 'Common Sense', in January 1987. It was an attempt at an accommodation with their republican enemies and, its authors believed, the only alternative to 'bloody civil war'. It proposed devolution with power-sharing but restricted to those who accepted Northern Ireland's right to exist. It also supported the idea of a written Constitution and a bill of rights to reassure further the minority. This suggested solution made little or no impact. A few influential nationalists showed some interest but the unionist leaders ignored it and the public, by and large, were unmoved by it. It failed to boost the electoral performance of loyalist paramilitary candidates; these were of poor quality, had little that was distinctive to offer voters, were perceived to have no solution to the issues raised by the Agreement and were closely identified with vicious sectarian violence. Most of the UDA members themselves had little interest in any political initiative. Their consuming interest was to avenge IRA violence by sustaining a high death count against the minority. (Nonetheless, the number of loyalist murders was consistently half or less the total of those committed by republicans in the late 1980s.) This response was confirmed by extensive leadership changes in the organisation during 1988-1990; all but one of its inner council members were then arrested or ejected. They were replaced, generally by those who were more ruthless and less well-known to the security forces.

The SDLP's Strategy after the Agreement

Predictably, the informal and sporadic inter-party talks held during the late 1980s made no measurable progress. The SDLP regarded both power-sharing and a significant Irish dimension as absolute pre-conditions for any internal political settlement while unionists would not fully accept either. But, in any case, John Hume had become primarily concerned to expand Dublin's influence in Ulster's administration in order to offset the permanent minority position of northern Catholics. The Anglo-Irish agreement had reduced further his interest in setting up any form of assembly or executive in the North. Both he and Éire's leaders recognised that under its terms successful devolution would directly result in the South's much valued consultative role being diminished. With other influential nationalists, he was anxious to build on the structures created by the accord – to move gradually towards full London/Dublin joint authority and, ultimately, unity. They hoped to pressurise Westminster into accepting Ireland's right to self-determination (i.e. unification) and that unionists could not be allowed to block or veto its achievement. The Agreement itself had raised expectations. After signing it, Garrett FitzGerald had declared: 'Britain has no interest in the continuing division of these islands.' This was especially true of the Labour Party, who regarded it as a step towards unity by consent.

Hume hoped to maximise nationalist bargaining strength by forming an even broader front than had emerged during the Forum in Dublin in 1983-84. His intention was to include not just constitutional nationalists throughout Ireland but also crucially Sinn Féin as well as Irish-American pressure groups and sympathetic elements within the EC. Their collective pressure would then be applied to the Conservative leadership and Britain's war weariness exploited. Within Northern Ireland the opportunities for such a strategy were beginning to improve. Gerry Adams, in particular, was responsive. During the Bobby Sands' by-election in

1981, he had already spoken of the need to form a broad 'anti-imperialist front'. By the mid-1980s, a constant theme of his speeches was his suggestion that the PIRA campaign might end if others could help find an alternative 'non-armed' means for the republican movement to achieve its political objective – 'Irish self-determination'.

Republican Attitudes and Prospects

Within Sinn Féin and the PIRA, pressures were emerging which made a cease-fire seem like a more acceptable option. A measure of war weariness was inevitable after almost twenty years of physical force and no prospect of military victory to compensate for the prolonged suffering and sacrifice entailed. This had already been expressed during the late 1970s by the Peace Movement (between 1969 and 1985 PIRA was responsible for more than half of the 2,400 killings in Northern Ireland; one quarter of their victims had been Catholic civilians). Though the campaign could, of course, be sustained, morale varied from area to area and there was a greater willingness within the leadership to consider alternative tactics. The ballot box/Armalite strategy had proved to be only a limited success and had failed to fulfil the hopes of its advocates. This was partly because the PIRA's continuing violence alienated the broader nationalist constituency. Yet it was difficult, if not impossible, for the Provisionals to 'fine-tune' their activities so as to avoid civilian casualties or actions which were seen as essentially sectarian. Its estimated 750 volunteers in the northern division confronted a combined security force strength of 30,000. They operated from no totally safe bases or liberated territory; surprise attacks on the widest possible range of targets therefore remained at the heart of their tactical approach. The resulting failure of Sinn Féin to become a more significant political force highlighted the PIRA's lack of an electoral mandate and, in turn, served to reinforce its view that physical force was essential.

In the North, the election held in 1983 represented the peak of the Sinn Féin party's support; thereafter, to Westminster's mounting relief, its share of the vote fell and stabilised at approximately half of the SDLP's percentage (in the Westminster elections of 1983 and 1987, the Sinn Féin vote dropped from 13.4 percent to 11.4 percent, whilst the SDLP percentage rose from 17.9 percent to 21.1 percent). Meanwhile, in southern Ireland, the Sinn Féin party's success at the polls during the hunger strike had fuelled expectations that it could win five Dáil seats within two further elections. It hoped then to hold the balance of power in the Dáil and use this pivotal position to compel southern leaders to exert pressure on British ministers to withdraw from the Six Counties. However, in the 1987 and 1989 elections, it attracted just 1.7 percent and 1.2 percent of the votes cast and won no seats. It performed even less well in local government elections; in 1991, just six of its candidates were successful out of a total of 883 councillors returned.

The changing perceptions within the republican movement opened up new opportunities, not only to unite all nationalist forces but also to end two decades of violence and use this prospect as a bargaining chip to extract concessions from Britain. For John Hume, it had a further advantage; he fully recognised that if Sinn Féin could be brought into negotiations, it would help stifle any future attempt to introduce a Six-County based scheme of devolution into the North. This had been the central plank of Westminster's policy there since the early 1970s; clearly, Adams and other republicans would never be party to such a settlement. Nonetheless, just such a settlement would almost certainly have received substantial moderate middle-ground, Catholic/Protestant support, so marginalising Sinn Féin further. Opinion surveys in 1986 and 1989 suggested that almost 80 percent of northern Catholics, and 60 percent of Protestants found power-sharing devolution with the United Kingdom acceptable: (for Catholics, it was by far their most popular first preference option). By the late 1980s, there is also evidence that southern attitudes were changing. Polls conducted in 1990 indicate that a substantial majority regarded an internal settlement in the North as the first priority, rather than unity and considered that Articles 2 and 3 of the 1937 Constitution should be amended. During a Dáil debate on these clauses, also in 1990, only Fianna Fáil supported their retention (a position it shared with the SDLP). Charles Haughey, still party leader, maintained that the Republic's claim to sovereignty over all thirty-two counties remained valid and that no internal solution to the Ulster question was feasible. He appealed for all Irish nationalists to stand together and speak with one voice. However, deputies from each of the other parties argued that the articles affronted unionists and thus impeded progress towards the primary objective – inter-community consensus on power-sharing governmental structures in the Six Counties. Furthermore, it was claimed that they legitimised the IRA campaign whilst doing nothing tangible to sustain the northern minority. Mary Robinson's election as president in November 1990 also suggested that the mould of Irish politics was being broken. She had earlier resigned from the Irish Labour Party in protest at the terms of the Anglo-Irish Agreement, which in her view treated northern unionists unfairly.

Hume/Adams talks

At the request of a third party, Hume met Adams for talks; negotiations continued over seven sessions between January and September 1988 (their first meeting in 1985 had lasted only minutes after Hume had refused to accede to the Sinn Féin wish that the proceedings be videoed). Both shared broadly similar viewpoints. They were opposed to any internal settlement in Northern Ireland, agreed on a principle that Ireland as a whole had a right to self-determination and therefore condemned any suggestion that unionists could veto moves towards unification. They believed that Britain should actively persuade the northern majority to accept unity. They disagreed, however, on one fundamental – the use of force. Hume argued that, given Britain's neutral attitude towards preserving Northern Ireland in the Union, physical force was unnecessary and indeed counter-productive. In his opinion, it positively delayed a solution and was divisive, alienating the unionists who had to be won over to accept political change. Adams, in contrast, was convinced that Britain still retained a selfish interest in the North and that the PIRA campaign remained the indispensable means to impel it to withdraw.

For the time being, the Hume/Adams talks ended in failure. But there was reason to believe that they might be successfully resumed in the future. Sinn Féin's northern leaders themselves recognised that Britain's policy towards the North was changing – the Anglo-Irish Agreement was tangible evidence of this. Rather than continue to denounce its terms, they began to cite them as proof of the effectiveness of the PIRA campaign. They were also aware of the danger that if Westminster made further concessions it would be other nationalist parties that would reap the benefit of the 'long war' conducted by the Provisionals. Sinn Féin could directly benefit itself only if it too was at the negotiating table. Contacts with the SDLP or the southern government might help open the door; in 1989, the new British Secretary of State, Peter Brooke, stated that he did not rule out talks with Sinn Féin if the violence ended.

The Brooke Talks

Brooke immediately initiated a protracted series of 'talks about talks' with local politicians which Sinn Féin promptly condemned for not being 'inclusive', i.e. not including its representatives. He was, in part, responding to international and British Labour Party pressure to act in the context of escalating violence. Also it was evident that the 1985 Accord had failed to bring peace and reconciliation. The need to amend or replace it was already being discussed by Dublin and London ministers; the estimated cost of Northern Ireland's 'Troubles' to both governments was then over £400 million yearly. Britain was also concerned to strengthen constitutional unionism. It was therefore gratified when, on 22 April 1991, the loyalist paramilitary leaders called a ceasefire; they did so to provide a favourable context for discussions, to indicate their desire for peace and to encourage the Provisionals to follow suit. After preliminary consultations between the local parties, hopes were raised when they agreed an agenda (on 30 April) based on John Hume's three-strand proposal (i.e. internal structures within the Six Counties to be agreed first,

North-South institutions next and finally those between Britain and Ireland). It was also accepted by all that 'nothing was agreed until everything was agreed'.

The inter-governmental conference set up under the agreement broke off its regular meetings for ten weeks from 26 April to allow time for formal inter-party negotiations to take place. These eventually began on 17 June 1991. The two unionist parties then proposed together that the 1985 accord be replaced with a limited measure of devolution, which included some provision for power-sharing but no Irish dimension. This submission held no attraction for the SDLP. It itself put forward no specific plans for internal structures for the North. Its main concern was to expand on the consultative role which the Republic had acquired in 1985. Predictably, by 16 July 1991, when the inter-governmental conference resumed its meetings, the talks process had ground to a standstill without making progress even on Strand 1.

The Mayhew Talks

The unionist leadership clamoured for further negotiations. Paramilitary violence was escalating. They were also anxious that talks should proceed before the imminent Westminster election, which the Labour Party (then strongly pro-Irish unity by consent) seemed set to win. Once more, the three-strand agenda was adopted but the negotiation process was soon disrupted. On 30 January 1992, Charles Haughey was forced to resign against the background of poor election results, successive scandals and mounting economic difficulties; on 6 February, Albert Reynolds, a leader without the same hard-line nationalist reputation, replaced him. A few months later, on 9 April, the British general election occurred. The Conservative party was re-elected under John Major's leadership (he had been Prime Minister since 22 November 1990) with a Commons majority of just twenty-one, so enhancing the influence of Unionist MPs in the Commons. In a cabinet reshuffle, Sir Patrick Mayhew became Secretary of State, replacing Brooke who had aroused unionist ire by singing 'My darling Clementine' on an RTE talk show hours after the murder of eight Protestant workmen by an IRA bomb at Teebane, County Tyrone, in Northern Ireland. As Attorney-General, Mayhew had criticised the southern government's handling of extradition cases and opposed the prosecution of eleven RUC officers on 'shoot to kill' charges.

IRA bombs in London on 10 April, in which three died, injected greater urgency into the inter-party talks when they reconvened nineteen days later. The unionist parties again sought to replace the agreement. They aimed to induce the Republic to accept the position of the Six Counties within the United Kingdom and to rescind Articles 2 and 3 of its Constitution (i.e. the South's claim to jurisdiction over the Six Counties). This they claimed would 'unlock the barrier' to greater North-South co-operation and deprive the IRA of its 'hunting licence'. The DUP and UUP still differed over the details of any future devolution scheme. But they asserted the right of the northern majority to determine the nature of both the political institutions within the Six Counties and the relationship between North and South. At the same time, they favoured cross-border co-operation in matters of mutual concern and again guaranteed the minority its civil liberties. The SDLP utterly opposed any such settlement and instead proposed the formation of an executive to govern the region, comprised of representatives from the British and Irish governments and from the EC. It was noticeable that, throughout, the Conservative ministers present expressed no preference for any particular form of constitutional settlement. In contrast, the Dublin delegates strove to have its functions expanded beyond those resulting from the 1985 accord; FitzGerald later criticised its representatives as being 'tactless and abrasive' towards the unionists, and generally lacking in clear purpose.

In November 1992, the Brooke-Mayhew talks ended without agreement. They had been characterised throughout by repeated deadlocks and highlighted the deepening chasm between the aspirations and policies of the Ulster unionists and the constitutional Irish nationalist parties, after twenty years of 'the Troubles'. The persistent violence continued to polarise opinion throughout 1991 and 1992; successive massive IRA bombs exploded in Belfast and a number of predominantly Protestant towns throughout the North, including Lisburn, Lurgan, Bangor and Coleraine. The loyalist paramilitaries reacted by increasing their random attacks on the minority who perceived this response as an attempt to coerce it into accepting unionist domination and British control. On 27 August 1992, Hugh McKibbon, a twenty-one year old, died. He was the 3,000th 'official' victim of 'the Troubles'.

In this context, the prospect of any political settlement in the North seemed remote. Secret negotiations between London and representatives of Sinn Féin and the PIRA (revealed to acute Conservative embarrassment in November 1993) had made no greater progress than the Brooke-Mayhew talks. The British government claimed that the Provisionals had initiated the discussions in February 1993, when they had indicated that the conflict was over and that they wished to be helped to end it. Adams rejected this account; he stated that contacts dated back to 1990 or before, that Britain had seemed ready to make major concessions and had then 'walked away' The sticking points seem to have been the republican demand for British withdrawal within three weeks and Britain's conditions that the violence end before formal talks could begin and that the majority in Northern Ireland must determine the area's political future.

Developments within the Republican Movement

At the time, Adams discounted current rumours of a possible cease-fire as 'unfounded speculation' whilst PIRA leaders themselves denied reports of internal strains over whether to call off the campaign. Nonetheless, pressures were mounting within Sinn Féin and the PIRA, to vary their tactics at least. In the April 1992 Westminster election, the Sinn Féin vote dropped to 10 percent of the total poll. The SDLP attracted 23 percent and Dr Joe Hendron defeated Adams in West Belfast; (Sinn Féin's victory in 1983 had been its only concrete electoral gain in twenty-five years.) The result suggested that war weariness was growing, and confirmed the limited and diminishing success of the ballot box/Armalite strategy. In addition, the physical force campaign, though recently intensified, was clearly reaching a military stalemate rather than opening up the prospect of outright victory. Britain's security forces were substantial, effective and apparently determined. According to the RUC, minority sympathy for violence was being weakened by the increased loyalist killing rate of Catholics. As a consequence, the Provisionals' activities were beginning to generate greater criticism than before and funds were declining. A cease-fire would at least ease tensions within the republican movement over tactics and falling support. At the same time, it might bring positive gains and, if these proved insufficient, provide scope for the renewal of the campaign without any further erosion of popular sympathy.

Moreover, there seemed genuine reason to believe that a political initiative might produce substantial results. Britain appeared to be in a more yielding mood, so making the continued use of force perhaps unnecessary. A speech by Brooke, possibly prompted by Hume, made a deep impression on republicans. He stated in November 1990 that Britain had no strategic or economic interest in Northern Ireland, that it would accept Irish unity if this had the backing of most people inside the Six Counties and that its presence was entirely due to the existence of a pro-Union majority there. He also indicated that if the IRA campaign ended, British troops would be withdrawn and talks follow on the agreed three-strand basis, with his government having no pre-selected constitutional preference. Clearly, he and his colleagues were experiencing pressures of their own. By 1993-94, annual government spending in the North had reached £7.5 billion. Moreover, successive opinion polls in Britain during 1991 and 1992 indicated that fewer than 30 percent believed the area should remain within the United Kingdom and up to 60 percent favoured the immediate withdrawal of British troops. Adams responded to Brooke's remarks by suggesting to the Conservatives that in these circumstances they should recognise Ireland's right to self-determination, actively persuade unionists to accept unity and, if necessary, overrule their resistance in order to bring it about. He appealed to both London and Dublin governments for 'open-ended discussions' and 'inclusive dialogue'; he and other Sinn Féin leaders were becoming convinced that both administrations wanted talks and stated that they themselves would be 'open, flexible and ready for compromise'. Adams also urged southern leaders to help provide Sinn Féin with a constitutional alternative to physical force to achieve its political objectives.

Reynolds was highly sympathetic in response. He had distractions of his own; cabinet disagreements forced an election in the South on 25 November 1992, but he survived in office despite a sharp drop in Fianna Fáil support. His coalition partners did, however, change from Progressive Democrat to Labour; Dick Spring, the Labour leader, was now given special responsibility for Northern Ireland. From first becoming Taoiseach, Reynolds had strongly favoured a further political initiative in the North, as had Haughey his predecessor. He believed that Britain had become more 'pliable' in its approach to the issue, especially after successive large PIRA bombs had exploded in the City of London in 1992 and 1993. In June 1993, he therefore submitted a draft inter-governmental declaration to Major in support of Irish self-determination (i.e. the right of the Irish people as a whole to decide on the political structures throughout all thirty-two counties). He was especially anxious to induce the Provisionals to abandon their campaign as a pre-condition and a prelude to Sinn Féin entering inter-party negotiations. From his republican contacts, he believed that they had first to be convinced of the positive benefits of ending the 'long war'. From the outset, he was kept fully informed of, and encouraged, a new initiative emerging in the North in early 1993.

CHAPTER 13

The Beginnings of the Peace Process

Father Alex Reid, a Redemptorist priest from Belfast, acting as an IRA go-between, informed John Hume that the campaign might end if Sinn Féin was brought into talks and a sufficient offer was made. In the immediate background, a Provisionals' bomb had exploded in a shopping area in Warrington, England, on 20 March, causing the death of two children. This action was universally condemned and sparked off a new and vibrant peace movement in Ireland. The SDLP leader had earlier appealed to PIRA to show 'moral courage' and also for Britain to produce a joint declaration with Dublin, in effect ending British sovereignty in the North. On 10 April he met Adams for 'extensive discussions'. They later issued a public statement in support of Ireland's right to 'national self-determination'. At their meeting, both shared the view that Britain needed to be pushed; they therefore supported the formation of a broad nationalist front comprised of the SDLP and Sinn Féin and fully supported by the southern government and Irish-American opinion. It was hoped that their collective pressure might compel Westminster to recognise Ireland's right to self-determination and persuade unionists to accept Irish unity, possibly imposing such a settlement on them. Hume believed that the prospect of an immediate cease-fire might serve as a possibly decisive inducement for Conservative ministers to act. In June 1993, the British Labour Party proposed joint authority between London and Dublin over the North for twenty years, as a prelude to unity.

There seemed every reason for this optimism. Acting

in support of Hume-Adams, Reynolds made contact with Irish-American bodies in mid-1993; these had considerable and growing influence within the Democratic Party. During his successful presidential campaign in 1992, Bill Clinton had already voiced concern at the 'wanton use of lethal force by the security forces' in the North. He had supported sending a peace envoy, applying pressure to ensure that fair employment practices were adopted there and the granting of a US visa to Adams. After further talks, Hume and Adams produced a joint statement on 25 September stating that their talks had now been completed and that Dublin had been given their conclusions. Hume spoke of 'hopeful signs' before setting off for Washington; he fully briefed the Irish government on all developments after his return on 7 October. He then spoke of a 'document' which was never made public. This contained the broad principles on which he and Adams had become convinced, after consultations with the IRA and Dublin, that a peace process could be established. It called for Britain to accept Irish self-determination and indicate its intention to withdraw from Ireland and override the unionist veto on national unity. Amidst rising republican expectations, the two nationalist leaders stated that their discussions had been suspended in order to permit Dublin and London to respond. On 20 November, they issued a final joint statement, stressing that Britain's response was crucial. The emerging broad nationalist consensus was more easily formed because Sinn Féin policy had changed. In 1987, it had demanded that British ministers commit themselves publicly to withdraw from the Six Counties within the 'lifetime of the British government'. But by 1993, it sought merely Britain's recognition of Ireland's right to self-determination, and willingness to persuade unionists to accept unity and work towards its ultimate withdrawal in co-operation with Dublin.

Impact of the Hume-Adams Document

In mid-October, the Hume-Adams initiative was endorsed by Nelson Mandela and opinion polls suggested that it was by then supported by over 70 percent of the southern electorate. Nonetheless, the fact of having talks with (and thus 'legitimising') Sinn Féin and the secrecy surrounding the whole process caused widespread irritation. It was strongly criticised by opposition parties in the Dáil and resulted in such tensions within the SDLP that Adams feared that his discussions with Hume would have to be aborted. Major, likewise, protested that he 'knew nothing' of the content of the negotiations. Amongst unionists, the mood was one of anger and outrage. After a period of relative quiescence, the violence reached new peak levels; in October, there were more fatalities than in any month for seventeen years. The loyalist paramilitaries were especially active, overtaking the PIRA killing rate for the first time since 1975 and protesting that Northern Ireland must remain intact within the United Kingdom. Already, on 12 January 1993, the UDA had stated that all elements in the 'pan-nationalist front', including members of the SDLP and the southern government, were legitimate targets. Paisley described the Hume-Adams initiative as 'the greatest threat to the Union since the Home Rule crisis of 1912'. The unionist parties resented the attempt to 'go over their heads' and suspected the worst. They broke off all contact with the SDLP for the duration of its bilateral talks. Such was their distrust that Mayhew, who had been attempting since the spring of 1993 to revive discussions on a three-strand basis aimed at devolution, abandoned the effort as 'counter-productive'. Both he and Major also energetically sought to reassure the northern majority. They stated publicly that Sinn Féin would not be permitted to enter future negotiations until the violence was over 'for real' and a 'sufficient period' had elapsed in which the party's good faith could be verified. They affirmed that there would be no change in the constitutional status of the Six Counties without the consent of a majority there and ruled out 'secret deals' with the supporters of violence as the price of a cessation.

The Downing Street Declaration

In late October, the Dublin government appeared to distance itself from the Hume-Adams document. This was partly because a sequence of vicious atrocities in the North had caused criticism of their initiative. Also, despite Reynolds urging that it represented a great opportunity for peace, and his warning about the risk of further IRA bombs on the British mainland, Major regarded it as 'not the right way to proceed'. His negative response was not least because of his tenuous Commons majority at Westminster. At Brussels, on 29 October, when the two premiers met to discuss their combined response, they agreed (the Taoiseach reluctantly) to issue a joint statement that 'initiatives could only come from governments', that majority approval was a precondition of change in the North but nonetheless that a PIRA cease-fire would elicit an imaginative response from them both. They also committed themselves to restart the peace process. On 3 November, they announced that they would work jointly on a 'framework for peace, stability and reconciliation'.

Subsequent weeks were characterised by leaks and rumours and also hard inter-governmental negotiations in which Major suspected Reynolds of trying to resurrect the Hume-Adams proposals. Eventually, on 15 December, the Downing Street Declaration was published, to the delight of southern ministers. They considered that their views had prevailed on most points and were optimistic from their northern republican contacts that it would satisfy the Provisionals. It was a broad statement of agreed principles regarding Ireland's future and was promoted as having the dynamic to bring peace (a more specific joint statement was to follow). Its stated objective was to help bring about agreement between the two political traditions in Ireland. The British government accepted in principle Ireland's right to self-determination and the need for change; this was a breakthrough for republicans, though, according to the Declaration, any move towards unity would require Northern Ireland's consent. Westminster reaffirmed that it had no selfish interest in the Six Counties, but, to Dublin's disappointment, made no commitment to persuade unionists to accept unity.

Mayhew believed that progress toward peace and reconciliation would now be possible through balanced accommodation on both sides in the context of inter-party talks. These would be based on the three-strand approach which, it was indicated, Sinn Féin could join after three months ('a decontamination period') of a permanent PIRA cease-fire. Reynolds's perspective was somewhat different. He was convinced that partition had failed and regarded the Declaration as 'a stepping stone'. He hoped that through negotiations, new cross-border institutions with executive powers could be agreed, leading ultimately to constitutional change and the achievement of unity, 'step by step'. In mid-December 1993, he was determined to press on 'to deliver peace' and to 'reel in' the Provisionals.

PIRA declare a Cease-Fire

Reynolds was hopeful that Sinn Féin and the PIRA would quickly endorse the Declaration and call a cease-fire. His optimism was based on its similarity to the Hume-Adams document, its massive popularity both in Ireland and in Britain and the palpable and almost universal public yearning for peace. However, throughout late 1993 and early 1994, the Provisionals sustained a high level of violence, much of it directed against loyalist districts. At the same time, they consulted their own supporters. They hesitated to endorse the December statement, both because it contained no British commitment to withdraw from Ireland and it again endorsed the principle that Irish unity was 'subject to the .... consent of a majority' in the North. The leadership called for 'direct and unconditional dialogue' with Britain and for 'clarification' on key points. There was opposition to a cease-fire amongst volunteers in Tyrone and Armagh and from hard-line fringe republican groups. Members of these were convinced that more bombs in London could compel Westminster into making the necessary concessions (a bomb at Bishopsgate on 24 April 1993 caused £350 million worth of damage).

Meanwhile, powerful pressures were applied to Sinn Féin and the PIRA to persuade them to institute a cease-fire. Reynolds regarded the British government's initial response to its requests as dilatory and abrasive. He therefore provided it with clarification (Major had at first refused), stressing the limited nature of the unionist veto on change in the North. He promised, if the violence ended, to lift the broadcasting ban on its spokesmen in the South, to begin releasing its prisoners and to help it obtain a US visa for Adams. He indicated that the cessation of the PIRA campaign would be the prelude to all-inclusive party talks which would offer Sinn Féin the opportunity to try to close the gap between the Hume-Adams document and the Declaration. His efforts were reinforced by Irish-American groups who committed themselves to use their influence to accelerate progress towards unity in Ireland if a cease-fire was declared. Hume, of course, also urged that his party would co-operate fully in the effort to realise Ireland's national right to self-determination. Above all, Adams argued that more progress would be made through a political initiative with SDLP, southern Irish and US backing than through the continued use of force. In any case he stressed that PIRA could, of course, preserve its organisation and its arms intact as well as the integrity of its ultimate aims.

As late as 24 July 1994, a Sinn Féin conference rejected the Declaration. Nonetheless, one month later they and the PIRA were persuaded that, through co-operation in a nationalist coalition, Conservative ministers could be compelled to concede their essential demands. Britain could be induced to accept in principle the need to end partition and positively work towards final withdrawal from Ireland. Thus a 'complete cessation of military operations' was declared, coming into effect at midnight on 31 August 1994; the timing of its announcement coincided with a vital debate in the Dáil, in the course of which Reynolds's government might otherwise have fallen. 'Inclusive negotiations' were eagerly anticipated by Sinn Féin.

Loyalist Cease-Fire

The issue remained whether the loyalist paramilitaries would follow suit. They had initially decided not to make any response to the Declaration until the position of the Provisionals was known. At first they had greeted the PIRA cessation with profound cynicism, suspecting that a secret deal had been struck with Westminster and/or that it was a temporary ruse to gain concessions from the British government. However they were reassured by Mayhew, Reynolds, the Washington administration and the text of the Declaration itself that there would be no change in the constitutional position of Northern Ireland without majority consent. Moreover, Major promised a referendum on the outcome of any future inter-party talks. Given the overwhelming public desire for peace, they were also convinced that further violence would gravely damage the unionist cause. They had, as well, frequently affirmed in the past that if the Provisionals called off their campaign they would do likewise. On 13 October, at a packed press conference, they declared a cease-fire as from midnight to last for as long as the republicans kept theirs. At the same time, they also expressed 'abject and true remorse' to the 'loved ones of all innocent victims over the past twenty-five years'.

Statistics of the Troubles

During those twenty-five years, 3,172 people died as a result of 'the Troubles' in Northern Ireland alone, dwarfing the total during the early 1920s (a further 235 were killed in Europe, including 119 in Britain and 100 in the Republic). Republican paramilitaries claimed the lives of an estimated 1,800 persons and the loyalists 880, in combination nine times more than the security forces. In addition, over 37,000 were injured, 25,000 of these civilians. There were 35,000 shooting incidents, 20,000 explosions and malicious fires and 19,000 armed robberies. Up to 1995, the British government had paid out £1,100 million in compensation for personal injury and damaged property. At present, it transfers £3.4 billion to Northern Ireland annually. If this support was withdrawn, unemployment in the region would rise by 20 percent within five years and its national income fall by roughly the same proportion. It would require a 25 percent tax increase in the Republic if its government were to assume Westminster's financial responsibilities there. At present, the security costs imposed by the northern 'Troubles' are almost three times more per head of population in the South than in Britain.

During the seventeen month cease-fire (September 1994 to February 1996), there were encouraging signs of sectional integration, returning normality and emerging civic unity. Within Northern Ireland, there was an effervescence of cross-community groups, organisations and activities; the first-ever Catholic deputy mayor of Belfast was elected and by November 1995, applicants from the minority to the RUC had risen by 9 percent. At the same time, administrative and trade contacts and travel between North and South increased dramatically. Nonetheless, it was from the outset unlikely that the cessation of violence would last, given the conflicting premises on which the PIRA and loyalist cease-fires were called.

Republican gains from the Cease-Fire

Sinn Féin and the PIRA took undoubted risks in ending the military campaign. There were physical dangers to the leaders; Peter Brooke described Adams as 'brave and courageous'. The longer peace held, the greater the PIRA's difficulty in reverting to physical force and the greater the likelihood of an internal split, unless sufficient political progress was made. The Sinn Féin leaders, however, did make decisive gains from the cease-fire. Their public profile and credibility were transformed by the ending of the broadcasting ban in Britain and in Ireland and the lifting of restrictions on their travelling to England and the United States, where they were also given permission to raise funds. They held meetings with government leaders in London, Dublin and Washington, which received global media attention. They participated in Reynolds's Forum for Peace and Reconciliation to discuss Ireland's future on an equal footing with other parties. In the northern local government elections in May 1993, the Sinn Féin vote had already recovered to 12.4 percent overall; in Belfast, it became the party with the largest share of the poll at 22.7 percent.

In addition, Sinn Féin and the PIRA made important security and political advances – prisoner releases, especially in the Republic, the removal of troops from daytime patrols in the North, some soldiers transferred back to Britain and the re-opening of cross-border roads. Above all, the framework document regarding Northern Ireland's future government, produced by London and Dublin in February 1995, was an attempt to devise institutions which would broadly satisfy the republican movement's demands. It made provision for an all-Ireland authority with radical executive powers. Adams claimed it as proof that partition had failed. unionists greeted it with deep hostility, arguing that Ulster was now set on a 'slippery slope' towards unity; the loyalist paramilitaries expressed 'fear and apprehension'.

Disappointment at Lack of Progress.

However, in other crucial areas, Sinn Féin leaders were surprised and disappointed by the lack of progress. The RUC remained unreformed and intact, and emergency legislation was not repealed. A few republican prisoners, about forty, were released within the United Kingdom itself. Above all, there were no inter-party talks inclusive of Sinn Féin, let alone signs of British withdrawal. Expectations in August 1994, that united nationalist pressure would quickly coerce Major into making vital political concessions, which would bring the 'end of British jurisdiction' in the North into sight, were unfulfilled. And indeed, there appeared to be good additional reasons why Britain should withdraw – her lack of any vital interest in the area, its drain on her resources, its complicating effect on her international relations and internal security and the fact that most of her electorate warmly supported taking the 'troops out'.

But countervailing factors also influenced the policies of the Conservative government. It was concerned that any precipitate British action could lead to a Bosnia-style civil war in the North. It did not wish to appear to be making concessions to PIRA blackmail. It also felt an obligation to respect the wishes of the majority community in Northern Ireland. This concern was heightened by its own diminishing majority at Westminster (21 in April 1992, only three by December 1995) and deepening internal party divisions over policy towards Europe. Both greatly increased the political leverage of the twelve Unionist MPs, especially as the UUP was more effectively led after David Trimble replaced James Molyneaux as leader in September 1995. Meanwhile the cohesion of the combined nationalist forces was weakened by the emergence of John

Bruton as Taoiseach in November 1994. Labelled 'John Unionist' by Reynolds in the Dáil, he and his party, Fine Gael, were certainly less amenable to the Hume-Adams approach than his predecessor and Fianna Fáil had been. At the same time, under the leadership of Tony Blair from May 1994, the British Labour Party supported all the key elements of Conservative policy throughout the cease-fire and moved away from its traditional and overwhelming commitment to Irish unity.

No All-Party Talks

Crucially, neither the British political leadership, Conservative and Labour nor the Ulster Unionists were convinced of the genuineness of the cessation of violence by the Provisionals. It was noted that they did not use the term 'permanent' in their cease-fire declaration nor did their Army Council ratify the decision – this was a pre-condition under their Constitution if it was to be both binding and lasting. Also their volunteers remained sporadically active after 31 August 1994, dispensing brutal beatings in Catholic areas (115 during the first twelve months of cease-fire), carrying out occasional killings within their own community and continuing their surveillance on potential future targets in Britain and the Six Counties. Their leaders from time to time threatened a return to violence; on 13 August 1995, Adams stated publicly that 'they [the PIRA] haven't gone away, you know'. Above all, the PIRA resolutely refused to decommission any of its arms, even though this was raised by Major as a precondition before Sinn Féin could enter all-party discussions. Unionist leaders had totally rejected participation in negotiations with republicans unless their goodwill had been established beyond all doubt: (e.g. by handing in their weapons).

The British government's position aroused widespread outrage and condemnation amongst nationalist leaders. Sinn Féin denounced it as a demand for the 'surrender' of the Provisionals, a delaying tactic and a denial of the party's mandate. Reynolds claimed that the British establishment was determined to 'undermine the peace process'. Hume demanded that Mayhew explain publicly why he was not talking to Adams.

The stalemate was eventually broken in November 1995, by the setting up of an international commission under US congressman George Mitchell to study and advise on the decommissioning of paramilitary arms. Its report on 26 January 1996 concluded that talks should be held in tandem with the handing over of weapons. It also laid down six principles for participation. These included the requirement that participants should be committed to using exclusively peaceful means to achieve political objectives and that all politicians involved should be willing to accept the outcome of the negotiating process. As no arms had been decommissioned, Major then adopted, without consulting Dublin, a Unionist/Alliance Party suggestion. (In doing so, he again outraged much nationalist opinion.) He proposed to hold an election to an Assembly in Northern Ireland on 30 May, after which all-party negotiations on political structures in the North would begin. The date set for the initiation of talks was 10 June 1996. Sinn Féin was to be admitted if a PIRA cease-fire was then in operation.

Prospects for Peace

On 4 February 1996 a massive bomb exploded in a car park at Canary Wharf, London, causing the death of two men, injuring 100 people and resulting in £85 million damage to property. The blast signalled the end of the IRA cease-fire. Its members blamed this outcome on the dilatoriness of the British government which it continued to regard as at the root of the conflict. Certainly, Major's slim majority had increased Unionist leverage at Westminster; to the Unionist leaders themselves the resumption of violence suggested that the cease-fire had merely been a tactic all along, conditional on the republicans getting their way.

For over a year the prospect of peace returning seemed exceedingly remote. Sporadic IRA activity continued. Initially it was confined to England, where the worst outrage occurred on 15 June 1996 when a large explosion devastated Manchester city centre. In October 1996, the campaign was renewed in Northern Ireland, beginning with two car bombs at Theipval Army Barracks, Lisburn. Ominously, this suggested that the IRA had abandoned any hope of progress in the peace process. It also inevitably placed enormous and sustained pressure on the Loyalist cease-fire which was from the outset conditional on the complete cessation of republican violence. Meanwhile, in public statements, Sinn Féin indicated that it would sign the Mitchell Principles. For its part, the IRA stated that the likelihood of a renewed 'unequivocal' cease-fire would be enhanced if, after calling it, republicans were admitted directly into the inter-party talks (ie, without any pre-condition regarding the prior decommissioning of their weapons).

During these months, the peace process progressed at a snail's pace. Forum elections were held under a complex system which guaranteed fringe group representation, including the women's movement and small Loyalist parties with links to paramilitaries. Despite Unionist hopes that the elected body would be directly involved in the negotiations, its function was downgraded to merely providing a reservoir from which members of the parties' negotiating teams would be drawn (in due course, its sessions became aimless and inconsequential). Sinn Féin campaigned vigorously in order to strengthen its mandate and so apply additional pressure for its admission to the talks. When these began on 10 June (with republicans excluded), little was achieved beyond the acceptance of Mitchell as chairman, and some agreement on procedures. In essence, they were stalled by the Unionist Party's insistence on partial IRA decommissioning as a pre-condition to Sinn Féin entry and its unwillingness to allow the issue to be dealt with by a special committee. This would have side-stepped the issue and enabled real discussion on the province's political future to proceed. In December, Major admitted that the process was 'stuck'. As a Westminster election was imminent, the talks were formally abandoned between 5 March and 3 June 1997.

In the background, the political atmosphere was poisoned by the issue of Orange Order marches, especially near Portadown where the Orangemen insisted on walking down their 'traditional' route – the Garvaghy Road – which was now fringed by a Catholic housing estate. Adams' statement, reported on RTÉ, that Sinn Féin was 'behind some residence groups', added to the difficulties of finding a solution. The government's decision to permit the parade to proceed, under police escort, on 11 July 1996 caused riots in nationalist districts, inflamed anti-RUC sentiment there and precipitated a widespread boycott of businesses owned by members of the Order. In retaliation, Loyalists picketed a Catholic church in Ballymena, County Antrim. The tense atmosphere generated by the annual 'marching season' helped inflate the Sinn Féin vote. In the general election (1 May 1997), the party won 16.1 percent of votes cast (the SDLP received 24.1 percent) and both Adams and McGuinness were returned; this was Sinn Féin's best result since the Troubles began. This apart, Northern Ireland was like a spectator at the historic contest: Tony Blair was already assured of becoming premier before a single vote had been counted in the six counties.

Even after the election, IRA violence continued unabated. On 9 May, a RUC constable was murdered in a Belfast bar, and two policemen were shot dead while on foot patrol in Lurgan five weeks later. But pressures to end the campaign mounted. Public expectations were raised by Labour's decisive victory, clearly its 147 majority left it free of Unionist influence. Even in October 1996, according to an opinion poll in the *Irish News* (a northern Nationalist paper), 94 percent of those questioned wanted a cease-fire, including 70 percent of Sinn Féin supporters. In these circumstances, John Hume's threat to 'look elsewhere' if a cease-fire was not called seemed credible. Moreover, by mid-1997, republican entry into talks after a credible cessation of violence had become acceptable to British politicians, providing Sinn Féin first signed the Mitchell Principles. This view had been held for some time in Washington and Dublin, as well as by the SDLP. Ahern's victory in the Dáil elections (6 June 1997) must have added to the appeal of entering the negotiations. He considered that his role as southern leader was to act as 'protector of the Nationalist people' in the north (an approach criticised by Bruton who favoured a more 'neutral' stance). By 23 June, Ahern and Blair had agreed a formula whereby decommissioning would be sidelined from the negotiations by creating a separate sub-committee to deal with the matter. At the same time, they issued an appeal to the IRA to call off its campaign so that republicans could enter the substantive inter-party discussions set to resume on 15 September, allowing time for a brief 'decontamination period'. Four weeks later, on 19 July, a cease-fire was called and was subsequently endorsed on 25 July by the republican prisoners.

The arrival of Sinn Féin at Stormont when the talks resumed immediately precipitated a DUP/UKUP walk-out. The UUP remained, however Trimble roundly denounced the 'relentless negativism' of his rivals. This response reflected his view that if Unionists refused to negotiate, the two governments would impose a pro-Nationalist solution on them.

The talks began inauspiciously. Trimble, facing strident criticism from hawks within his party, initially refused to negotiate 'face to face' with Sinn Féin (though they both attended plenary sessions). In October, he stated publicly that he felt 'no expectation of an agreement'. Similarly, Sinn Féin's action in signing the Mitchell Principles was condemned by some; the IRA indicated that it would 'have problems' with a number of them. There were also ominous reports of defections to fringe republican groups, particularly in south Armagh and around Dundalk in the Republic. One of these, the Continuity IRA, carried out a series of massive bomb attacks on northern towns. Meanwhile, despite the provisional and Loyalist cease-fires, punishment beatings by both paramilitary groups continued unabated (44 occurred between 19 July and 7 November 1997) and also, occasionally, murders. These resulted in Sinn Féin and one of the Loyalist parties being expelled briefly from the negotiations. Nonetheless, the violence was on a lesser scale than in the past.

Despite some republican hostility to the 'partitionist talks', the movement reaped benefits virtually immediately from its involvement. Adams' visa to the United States was renewed and he was free to raise funds during his visit, also IRA members currently on trial in America were not extradited to Britain. The southern government began the early release of its republican prisoners. At Westminster, Labour ministers began to dismantle Britain's emergency legislation (notably abandoning the power to intern). The number of troops in the province was reduced and the frequency of their patrols lowered. Moreover, the negotiations themselves held out the prospect of seats for Sinn Féin in any future regional executive. Meanwhile, Nationalists generally welcomed the Blair government's 'confidence building measures'. These included an inquiry into Bloody Sunday, the setting up of a commission on police reform and the launching of an 'equality strategy' aimed at reducing Catholic unemployment.

At the talks themselves, slow but meaningful progress was being made. On 9 September, Sinn Féin signed the Mitchell Principles. In late October the UUP conference officially endorsed Trimble's participation. Before this, delegates from both parties had agreed that an International Commission should be established to deal with decommissioning, hitherto the gravest obstacle to political progress. Thereafter, the crucial element in accelerating the process was the active intervention by London and Dublin. The two governments produced Heads of Agreement documents (12 January 1998) to kick-start the negotiations after Christmas, backed up by further detailed proposals two weeks later. Subsequently, at a critical juncture, they imposed a time-table and a strict deadline on the parties by which time agreement was to have been reached.

Senator Mitchell proved to be a skilful and resourceful chairman. He introduced a new, streamlined format whereby each of the ten parties involved nominated two delegates to represent them in the discussions. The

Mitchell Document, which he produced at 12.30am on Tuesday 7 April (with the approval of Blair and Ahern), provided a framework for the eventual agreement. Subsequently, personal involvement by the British premier and the Taoiseach in the final, nail-biting sessions, which lasted well into the night under the full glare of the international media, was the remaining vital ingredient which helped secure a successful outcome.

The historic Belfast Agreement (10 April 1998) makes provision for the election of a 108-seat assembly which is to have powers devolved from Westminster over matters such as economic development, education, health and agriculture. Its key decisions require cross-community support; a statistical formula is incorporated to ensure that each has significant backing from the representatives of both traditions. Parties with sufficient seats are automatically entitled to hold ministerial office; power-sharing is thereby guaranteed. A north-south council, comprised of members of the northern executive and the Irish government, must be established for mutual consultation on cross-border, policy cooperation. Whether it will have executive powers is as yet unclear. A new British-Irish Intergovernmental Conference will replace existing arrangements under the Anglo-Irish Agreement, and will 'intensify cooperation between the two governments' on matters such as security, rights, justice, prisons and policing. A provision is included to amend Articles 2 and 3 of the Republic's constitution so that it embodies the principle of consent within Northern Ireland to any future change in its status. In addition, prisoners in paramilitary organisations on cease-fire are to be released over the next two years and the policing system is to be reformed. Civil rights are guaranteed. Signatories also committed themselves 'to use any

influence they may have to achieve the decommissioning of all paramilitary arms within the next two years'.
Blair wrote to Trimble, on 10 April, reassuring him that
'in our view ... [it] ... should begin straight away'.

The Agreement was greeted with widespread
euphoria, tinged with disbelief. It certainly marks a historic opportunity for a new beginning in Irish political
life, it lays the basis of an agreed Ireland arguably for
the first time. It has the support within Northern Ireland
of a political spectrum ranging from Sinn Féin to the
fringe Loyalist parties linked to paramilitaries, while
also commanding the full backing of the governments
in London, Dublin and Washington. It is rooted in compromise and mutual consent and recognises fully the
rights and aspirations of both traditions – they can,
within the institutions it envisages, live and share
power together in peace, stability and security.

Since 10 April 1998, the Agreement has acquired the
legitimacy of democratic approval. In a referendum
(held on 23 May 1998), it was supported by 71 percent
of those who voted in the north and 95 percent in the
south – 94 percent of the Irish people overall. Almost 75
percent of the members of the Ulster Unionist Council
have backed it, and the Sinn Féin Árd Fheis has given it
a guarded welcome. The assembly, elected on 25 June,
ratified the new governmental structures based on the
Agreement, submitted to it by the first minister desig-
nate, David Trimble, and his deputy, Seamus Mallon of
the SDLP. These provide for a twelve-member executive, ten departments and the formation of six
north-south bodies. The courage shown and progress
made by local Nationalist and Unionist leaders was
acknowledged by the award of the Nobel Peace Prize
jointly to Trimble and John Hume (10 December 1998).
Meanwhile, the perpetrators of a car bomb atrocity at

Omagh, County Tyrone (15 August), which killed 29 people – mainly women and children – were condemned by all but the fringe republican group responsible for it. Adams stated: 'Sinn Féin believe the violence we have seen must be over for all of us now, a thing of the past, over, done with and gone'.

Though progress has undoubtedly been made, the Agreement may yet become derailed. Cynics have argued from the outset that, in the long term, the Agreement cannot satisfy the mutually conflicting positions and expectations deriving from it in Northern Ireland. Its Unionist supporters believe it strengthens the union, which is why some republicans are so hostile to it. Some Sinn Féin supporters believe it contains a dynamic towards a united Ireland, which is the reason why the DUP and UKUP oppose it. Already, some critical divisions have appeared regarding its implementation, particularly in relation to paramilitary weapons, an issue successfully fudged during negotiations hitherto. Sinn Féin constantly criticise Trimble for the long delay in appointing an executive and demand to be given the two seats on it that their mandate entitles them to. They utterly reject any suggestion that their entry into government should be conditional on the IRA decommissioning some of its arms. They argue that such a requirement criminalises the IRA, implies that it was to blame for the past thirty years of violence and is tantamount to a demand for surrender. They also stress, with justification, that no such obligation is contained in the text of the Agreement and urge that it is more important that the guns remain silent than that they should be handed over. If compliance was attempted, the republican movement might well split and the cease-fire collapse.

For his part, Trimble makes the dubious claim that

the Agreement does contain a commitment to decommission. What is, however, almost certain is that if he proceeds to set up an executive which includes Sinn Féin, his position as Unionist Party leader will crumble. When accepting the Nobel Prize, the Unionist leader appealed: 'All I have asked is for a credible beginning [to the hand-over of arms], that they say the war is over. That is not too much to ask for, nor too much to ask that the reformist party of nationalism support me in this'.

The popular euphoria at the time of the Agreement has diminished since. This is partly due to the persistence of both Loyalist and republican paramilitary assaults – described in *The Irish Times* as 'targeted terrorist terror'. Thus between 10 April and 20 December, a total of 55 people were beaten, 47 shot and 193 intimidated into leaving their homes. William Hague, the Conservative Party leader, has urged that in reply the steady flow of prisoner releases should be halted in the hope of terminating these abuses. They are sustained at a high level partly to substantiate claims that law and order has broken down due to inadequate policing; the issue of police reform remains highly sensitive and deeply divisive. In addition, since the Agreement, Loyalist groups have sustained a low level campaign, characterised as before by viciousness and sectarianism. There are also constant media reports of the defection of members and leaking of arms from the IRA to fringe republican groups not on cease-fire and sporadically active. It is a depressing fact that despite the widespread condemnation of the Omagh atrocity, no one has been charged with the outrage. Indeed, charges have been brought in just 29 percent of the 1,940 murders attributed to republicans over the past thirty years, likewise, charges have been brought in only 50 percent of the 888 killings attributed to Loyalists in the same period (*Belfast Telegraph*, 19 January 1999). Meanwhile, the Orange Order continues to demand that it be permitted to march along 'traditional' routes, including through Catholic areas where its presence is offensive. The issue continues to pollute the political atmosphere.

The two Ulster communities have inherited and, until now at least, retained deeply divergent political aspirations. Northern Nationalists regard Ireland as one nation, divided in 1920 by Britain, which has since been responsible for keeping it divided. Unionists claim that Ireland contains two distinct peoples, they have criticised Nationalists for their refusal to recognise this, and their failure to accord to them their right to self-determination. They have not regarded themselves as a 'tradition' within the Irish nation, nor have they regarded Britain's support as other than unreliable. The Agreement contains the potential to break this ancient mould. But it could still become impaled on the rocks of ideological absolutism, paramilitary violence and deep-seated sectarian prejudice. Orange tribalism and the continuing viciousness of the fringe Loyalist paramilitary groups do not augur well. Meanwhile, republican hawks retain the objective of breaking Britain's will. They no doubt still possess the capacity in arms, volunteers and support to resume their campaign of physical force. Certainly, to abandon it permanently would drastically reduce their political leverage. To do so before attaining their goals would leave their members feeling betrayed, the death and sacrifices of the past thirty years would seem to have been in vain. At present, by far the most hopeful sign is the attempt by some local leaders to rise to that higher level of statesmanship which does not merely pander to its own supporters, but dares to chip away at their prejudices.